Scrum - A practical Guide

Your guide to the Agile Development Approach
that dominates modern software development

Michael Carter

MCAREL Consulting

Superior Advisory services for our dev to customers

Table Of Contents

Chapter 1.1

An overview of Agile principles, values, and its significance in today's dynamic project environment

So let's start by defining this magic dust called Agile that helps us deliver software projects. At its core, Agile is more than just a methodology or a set of practices for software development; it's a mindset, a way of thinking and, above all, a way of working that champions flexibility, collaboration, and customer satisfaction.

Born out of a need to break free from the traditional, rigid, and often slow-paced waterfall model, Agile emerged as a breath of fresh air for developers and project teams worldwide. It was like someone said, "Enough! There's got to be a better way to do this," and lo and behold, the Agile Manifesto was conceived in 2001. This manifesto, crafted by 17 software developers, laid down four fundamental values and twelve principles that aimed to streamline project management and software development.

So, what are these values and principles that make Agile what it is? Let's have a quick look at.

The Agile Values:

1. Individuals and interactions over processes and tools: Agile puts people first. It's the idea that a well-oiled team, communicating openly and frequently, is more effective than the most sophisticated tools or stringent processes.

2. Working software over comprehensive documentation: This doesn't mean documentation isn't important; it's just that delivering a working product to the customer takes precedence. Agile advocates for "just enough" documentation that supports the development process without hindering it.

3. Customer collaboration over contract negotiation: Agile encourages ongoing interaction with the customer throughout the project. It's about embracing changes, even late in development, to ensure the end product truly meets the customer's needs.

4. Responding to change over following a plan: The only constant is change, especially in today's fast-moving project environments. Agile is about being flexible and adaptable, ready to pivot when necessary.

And the significance?

In today's dynamic project environments, the Agile approach is more relevant than ever. It allows teams to deliver value faster, with higher quality and predictability, and greater aptitude to respond to change. It's not just about software development anymore; Agile principles have found their way into various industries, revolutionising the way projects are managed and products are developed. Agile is constantly evolving, and to make the most of these developments, it's important for you to understand the value each practice gives you, whether it's the latest and greatest or something you've been following for a while.

Implementing Agile can lead to enhanced team productivity and morale, improved customer satisfaction, and a more efficient project management process. It's about creating a culture where feedback is valued, failures are seen as learning opportunities, and the focus is on delivering tangible, valuable outcomes to customers.

Understanding Agile is about recognising the shift from a traditional, linear approach to a more flexible, iterative process. It's about embracing change, focusing on collaboration, and putting the customer at the heart of the project. In today's ever-evolving project landscape, Agile offers a beacon of adaptability, efficiency, and effectiveness.

So, whether you're a seasoned Agile enthusiast or just starting to dip your toes into this dynamic world, remember that it's all about embracing change, fostering collaboration, and continually striving to deliver value. Agile isn't just a methodology; it's a journey, an ethos, and perhaps a bit of a revolution.

Chapter 1.2 - The Agile Manifesto

A deep dive into the Agile Manifesto, interpreting its four core values and twelve principles

The Agile Manifesto! It's a bit like the secret sauce behind some of the most dynamic and successful project teams out there. Created by a group of 17 forward-thinking software developers back in 2001, this manifesto laid the groundwork for a whole new way of working on software projects. So, let's dive deep into the heart of the Agile Manifesto, exploring its four core values and twelve guiding principles.

Firstly, the Agile Manifesto is built around four key values that essentially turned the traditional project management approaches of the time on their heads. The core values were defined as :

Individuals and interactions over processes and tools

This one values human communication and collaboration above all those fancy tools and stringent processes. It's the idea that a well-oiled team can achieve more than the sum of its parts when its members actually talk to each other and work together effectively.

Working software over comprehensive documentation

Remember those days when you'd drown in paperwork before writing a single line of code? Agile says, "No more!" It's all about getting a working product out there for feedback rather than waiting until everything is dotted in the documentation. Documentation is still important in Agile processes, but the key here is sufficient documentation where that documentation adds value.

Customer collaboration over contract negotiation

Instead of locking everything down with contracts up front, Agile encourages ongoing dialogue with customers. This way, you can adapt to their needs as the project evolves rather than sticking rigidly to a plan that might not serve them in the end.

Responding to change over following a plan

The world changes rapidly, and Agile recognises that. This value is all about being flexible and ready to pivot when necessary, rather than blindly adhering to a plan that's become outdated.

So those are the four core values. These are then fleshed out by twelve principles on which Agile methods generally try to base themselves. So lets talk about the

The Twelve Principles Behind the Agile Manifesto

1. Our highest priority is satisfying the customer through early and continuous delivery of valuable software.

It's all about getting that product into the customer's hands early and then improving it from there. It not only give the client something they can use, but the feedback gained is invaluable.

MCAREL Consulting

2. Welcome changing requirements, even late in development.
Agile projects are all about flexibility; changes aren't just expected; they're embraced.

3. Deliver working software frequently, from a couple of weeks to a couple of months, with a preference for a shorter timescale.
Regular updates mean you're always moving forward and keeping the customer involved.

4. Business people and developers must work together daily throughout the project.
It's a team sport, folks. Everyone needs to be informed and able to collaborate closely.

5. Build projects around motivated individuals. Give them the environment and support they need, and trust them to get the job done.
This is about empowering the team, giving them what they need, and then stepping back to let them shine.

6. The most efficient and effective method of conveying information to and within a development team is face-to-face conversation.
Despite our digital age, nothing beats a good old discussion for clearing things up quickly.

7. Working software is the primary measure of progress.
If it's working, you're winning. Simple as that.

8. Agile processes promote sustainable development.
It's all about keeping a steady pace and avoiding burnout while maintaining velocity.

9. Continuous attention to technical excellence and good design enhances agility.
Quality matters. A well-crafted product is easier to adapt and extend.

10. Simplicity, "the art of maximising the amount of work not done," is essential.
Why complicate things? If it doesn't need doing, bin it. Focus on what truly adds value. Or, as we used to say, "YAGNI" or "You Ain't Gonna Need It."

11. The best architectures, requirements, and designs emerge from self-organising teams.
Give the team freedom, and they'll come up with solutions you never dreamed of.

12. At regular intervals, the team reflects on how to become more effective, then tunes and adjusts its behaviour accordingly.
It's all about learning and improving as you go, always striving to do better.

So, there you have it, the Agile Manifesto in all its glory. It's not just about doing things faster; it's about doing things better, with more flexibility, better communication, and a stronger focus on delivering real value. Whether you're building software, managing projects, or just looking to work more effectively, there's a lot we can all learn from the Agile Manifesto.

Chapter Summary

The Agile Manifesto is a foundational document created by 17 software developers in 2001, setting the tone for a new method of working on software projects. It comprises four core values that revolutionized traditional project management:

- Individuals and interactions over processes and tools, emphasizing human communication and collaboration.
- Working software over comprehensive documentation, prioritizing functional products over exhaustive paperwork.
- Customer collaboration over contract negotiation, advocating for ongoing dialogue and adaptability.
- Responding to change over following a plan, promoting flexibility and adaptation to evolving needs.

These values are further elaborated through twelve principles that underpin Agile methodologies:

- Customer satisfaction through early and continuous software delivery.
- Embracing changing requirements even late in development.
- Delivering working software frequently to maintain progress and customer involvement.
- Ensuring daily collaboration between businesspeople and developers.
- Empowering motivated individuals, providing support, and trusting them to excel.
- Emphasizing face-to-face conversations for effective information exchange.
- Using working software as the primary indicator of advancement.
- Promoting sustainable development to avoid burnout and maintain pace.

- Continuous attention to technical excellence and good design for enhanced agility.
- Embracing simplicity to focus on valuable work and avoid unnecessary tasks.
- Encouraging self-organizing teams to devise innovative solutions.
- Regular reflection and adjustment to improve team effectiveness continually.

The Agile Manifesto encourages a focus on delivering value, fostering flexibility, enhancing communication, and improving efficiency across software development and project management endeavors.

Introduction to Scrum

2.1: What is Scrum?

Introduction to Scrum as an Agile Framework, its origins, and How It differs from traditional project management methodologies.So, what is Scrum?

To me, Scrum! It's like the superhero of the Agile world, swooping in to save projects from the perils of inefficiency and disarray. If you're diving into the realms of Agile methodologies, understanding Scrum is akin to holding the key to a treasure chest of project management wisdom. So, let's embark on this exploratory journey together, shall we?

Scrum is not just a methodology but a framework for managing and completing complex projects. Originating in the software development industry, it has since spread its wings across various fields, proving its versatility and effectiveness. At its core, Scrum is built on the Agile philosophy, which favours flexibility, collaboration, and the delivery of value in quick, iterative cycles known as "sprints."

The genesis of Scrum can be traced back to a 1986 paper by Hirotaka Takeuchi and Ikujiro Nonaka, where they described a "rugby" approach to product development – moving forward as a unit, passing the ball back and forth. This rugby analogy laid the groundwork for what would become Scrum. It officially got its name and more defined structure in the early 1990s, thanks to the efforts of Ken Schwaber and Jeff Sutherland, who are considered the fathers of Scrum. They presented Scrum as a formal process at OOPSLA '95, and since then, it has evolved into one of the most popular Agile methodologies.

How Scrum works.

Scrum is predicated on a simple set of roles, responsibilities, and meetings (ceremonies) that help teams manage their work. The framework divides teams into small, cross-functional units that work in time-boxed sprints, usually lasting two to four weeks. Every iteration (or Sprint as it is known in Scrum) begins with a Sprint planning meeting and ends with a Sprint review and Sprint retrospective, ensuring continuous improvement. The meetings provide an opportunity for the team to think about what went well and the outcome/deliverables from the previous sprint and feed those findings into a plan for the next sprint.

Scrum Project Roles

The Product Owner

Represents the stakeholders and the voice of the customer. Responsible for defining the product's features and prioritising the work to be done. (Product Owner is the term I've seen used most for this role, so we'll stick with that.)

The Scrum Master

Acts as a facilitator for the team and the product owner. They ensure that the team follows Scrum processes and practices and remove any obstacles(commonly known as blockers) that might hinder their progress.

The Development team

A self-organising, cross-functional group, responsible for delivering the product increments at the end of each sprint.

Scrum Ceremonies

Scrum ceremonies are designed to ensure communication, collaboration, and continuous progress. These include: (we'll go into more detail later on in the book).

Sprint Planning

Defining what can be delivered in the next sprint and how the work will be achieved (the user story is the currency of choice in software projects when determining this).

Daily Scrum (Stand-up)

A brief daily meeting to discuss progress, plan for the day, and identify any impediments.

Sprint Review

This is held at the end of each sprint to examine the increment and groom the product backlog if needed.

Sprint Retrospective

A meeting to discuss the past sprint and identify improvements for the next sprint.

Scrum Artifacts

Scrum also introduces several artifacts to help manage work and ensure transparency.

Product Backlog

An ordered list of user stories detailing requirements for everything that might be needed in the planned system, constantly evolving and managed by the product owner.

Sprint Backlog

A set of User Stories, selected from the Product Backlog, to be completed in the current sprint, along with a plan for delivering the product increment and achieving the sprint goal.

Increment

The sum of all the product backlog stories completed during a sprint. These must be in a usable condition. (Generally, an increment represents a release of code to production; this can include work from one or more sprints.)

How Scrum Differs from Traditional Project Management Methodologies

Traditional project management methods, such as waterfall, are linear and sequential. Every phase of the project must be completed before proceeding to the next. This often leads to rigidity and makes it difficult to incorporate changes once the project is underway.

Scrum, on the other hand, embraces change. It acknowledges that customer needs can evolve and that new information can emerge, affecting the project's direction. This flexibility allows Scrum teams to adapt rapidly without derailing the entire project.

Moreover, Scrum fosters a high level of team collaboration and empowerment. Unlike traditional methodologies, where decisions are often made at the top, Scrum encourages team members to make decisions and take ownership of the work. This not only boosts morale but also leads to more innovative solutions and a higher-quality product.

In essence, Scrum is about adapting, evolving, and delivering value quickly. It's a framework that not only transforms how projects are managed but also changes the culture of the organisations that adopt it, promoting a more dynamic, collaborative, and efficient approach to work. Whether you're building software, launching a marketing campaign, or creating new products, Scrum offers a powerful, proven way to achieve your goals and delight your customers. However, one thing to note. If you followed the treatment of the Agile Manifesto, you'll have noticed the Core value of "Working Code over comprehensive documentation.". Scrum doesn't specifically have this value as Scrum is a product methodology, i.e.
you can organise teams other than software teams using Scrum. However, if you're using Scrum to produce a software product, you should be adhering to this value.

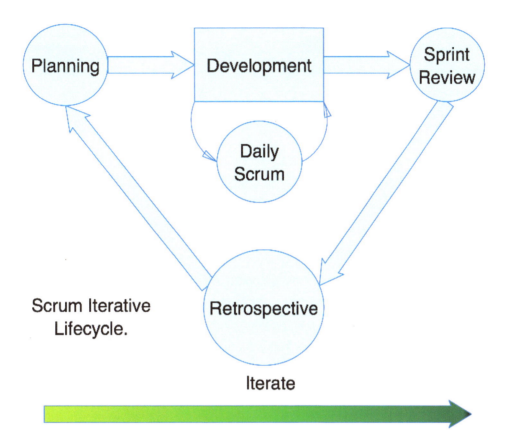

Scrum Iterative Lifecycle.

Iterate

Recap on Scrum

So, what is Scrum? To me, Scrum! It's like the superhero of the Agile world, swooping in to save projects from the perils of inefficiency and disarray. If you're diving into the realms of Agile methodologies, understanding Scrum is akin to holding the key to a treasure chest of project management wisdom. So, let's embark on this exploratory journey together, shall we?

- Introduction to Scrum: Scrum is not just a methodology but a framework for managing and completing complex projects. Originating in the software development industry, it has since spread its wings across various fields, proving its versatility and effectiveness. At its core, Scrum is built on the Agile philosophy, which favors flexibility, collaboration, and the delivery of value in quick, iterative cycles known as "sprints."

- Origins of Scrum: The genesis of Scrum can be traced back to a 1986 paper by Hirotaka Takeuchi and Ikujiro Nonaka, where they described a "rugby" approach to product development moving forward as a unit, passing the ball back and forth. It officially got its name and more defined structure in the early 1990s thanks to the efforts of Ken Schwaber and Jeff Sutherland.

- How Scrum Works:

- The framework divides teams into small, cross-functional units that work in time-boxed sprints, usually lasting two to four weeks.

- Every iteration (or Sprint as it is known in Scrum) begins with a Sprint planning meeting and ends with a Sprint review and Sprint retrospective, ensuring continuous improvement.
- The key roles in Scrum:
    - Product Owner/Manager
    - Scrum Master
    - Development Team
- The Scrum Ceremonies:
    - Sprint Planning
    - Daily Scrum (Stand-up)
    - Sprint Review
    - Sprint Retrospective
- Scrum Artefacts:
    - Product Backlog
    - Sprint Backlog
    - Increment

- How Scrum Differs from Traditional Project Management Methodologies:
    - Traditional project management methods, such as waterfall, are linear and sequential. This often leads to rigidity and makes it difficult to incorporate changes once the project is underway.
    - Scrum, on the other hand, embraces change and fosters a high level of team collaboration and empowerment.

- Core Value: Scrum doesn't specifically have the Core value of "Working Code over comprehensive documentation" as it is a product methodology. However, when using Scrum to produce a software product, it is recommended to adhere to this value.

2.2: Benefits of Scrum
Exploring the advantages of adopting Scrum for project management and product development.

We've used the analogy before, but Scrum is like the Swiss Army knife of the project management world. It's versatile and packed with features that can tackle almost any challenge thrown its way. As we venture into the realm of Scrum, let's unpack the myriad of benefits it brings to project management and product development. So, grab a cup of tea, and let's delve into why Scrum might just be the game-changer you've been looking for.

First off, Scrum thrives on change. Unlike traditional methodologies that treat change as a foe, Scrum welcomes it with open arms. In the fast-paced world we live in, the ability to adapt swiftly to market shifts, customer feedback, and emerging trends is invaluable. Scrum's iterative nature allows teams to pivot quickly, ensuring that the final product is as relevant and valuable as possible. It's like being able to reroute your satellite navigation in real time to avoid traffic jams on the way to your destination.

Enhanced Product Quality

Scrum's emphasis on regular reviews and iterations accelerates development and significantly boosts product quality. Each sprint ends with a shippable product increment, allowing for immediate feedback and adjustments. This continual refinement process ensures that quality is baked into the product from the outset, rather than being an afterthought. It's akin to perfecting a recipe by tasting and tweaking as you go rather than waiting until the end to realise you've added too much salt. The focus on prioritising features and committing to building only the most needed items first is key to avoiding distractions and concentrating on high-quality code.

Improved Customer Satisfaction

At the heart of Scrum is the focus on delivering real value to customers early and often. By involving stakeholders in the process and prioritising their needs, Scrum ensures that the product evolves in a direction that's genuinely useful to them. This collaborative approach not only results in products that meet or exceed expectations but also strengthens the relationship between the team and its customers. Misunderstandings are identified earlier and, in many cases, eliminated altogether. The customers see the product being built and are available to give instant feedback to the developers. They also get to use the product at a much earlier point in the project.

Increased Project Visibility

Scrum promotes transparency throughout the development process. Regular meetings, such as daily stand-ups and sprint reviews, ensure that everyone is up to speed and potential issues are flagged early on. This visibility allows stakeholders to track progress in real-time, making it easier to manage expectations and make informed decisions. Product Owners are involved in every aspect of the delivery. They can provide regular feedback to the project team and to their management structure. Plus, at the end of every sprint, working code is delivered, and the emerging system becomes a reality in front of the customer's eyes. However, this visibility can be a double-edged sword for developers. If the project fails to meet its sprint goals, this will become immediately apparent to the customer. However, on the whole, project visibility and transparency are good things that customers generally value.
They make it more likely the customer will work with the team to resolve issues that do arise.

Higher Team Morale

Scrum teams are self-organising and empowered to make decisions, which can lead to higher motivation and job satisfaction. The framework's collaborative nature fosters a strong sense of ownership and accountability, as every team member has a crucial role in the project's success. Plus, the regular achievement of milestones and the ability to see the impact of one's work can be incredibly rewarding. It's the difference between being a cog in a machine and being part of a close-knit team on a mission.

Faster Time to Market

With Scrum, the focus is on delivering a working product in short cycles, dramatically reducing the time to market. This rapid delivery capability enables organisations to take advantage of emerging business opportunities and stay ahead of their competition. It's the business equivalent of being the first to discover a shortcut that gets you to the market square before everyone else, allowing you to set up your stall and start selling while others are still on their way.

Better Management of Risks and Priorities

Scrum's iterative approach and regular feedback loops make it easier to identify and manage risks earlier in the process. Additionally, by prioritising work based on value and urgency, teams can ensure that they're always focusing on the tasks that matter most. This means that even if the project faces unexpected hurdles, you're well-equipped to handle them without derailing your entire schedule. It's like navigating a tricky obstacle course with the agility and foresight to avoid pitfalls and stay on track.

Cost Control

By concentrating on delivering the most valuable features first and allowing for changes along the way, Scrum can help control project costs. Waste is minimised as the team avoids spending time on features that won't make it into the final product or don't add significant value. In essence, Scrum ensures that every dollar spent moves you closer to your goal, rather than being squandered on misaligned objectives.

Adopting Scrum can transform the way you manage projects and develop products. It's a holistic framework that not only optimises your processes but also aligns your team, delights your customers, and delivers tangible value at every turn. Whether you're a start-up navigating your first product launch or a seasoned enterprise looking to inject agility into your projects, Scrum offers a proven, flexible, and effective approach to achieving success. So, why not give it a whirl? The benefits, as we've seen, are well worth the leap.

MCAREL Consulting
Superior Advisory services for Guidew to Customers

To summarise

- The benefits of the Scrum module are numerous and can have a significant impact on project management and product development:

  - Flexibility and Adaptability: Scrum welcomes change and allows teams to adapt swiftly to market shifts, customer feedback, and trends.
  - Enhanced Product Quality: Regular reviews and iterations result in higher product quality with immediate feedback and adjustments.
  - Improved Customer Satisfaction: Scrum focuses on delivering value early and involving stakeholders, leading to products that meet expectations.

  - Increased Project Visibility: Promotes transparency, tracks progress in real-time, involves stakeholders, and delivers working code at the end of each sprint.
  - Higher Team Morale: Self-organizing teams lead to higher motivation and job satisfaction with a strong sense of ownership and accountability.
  - Faster Time to Market: Delivering a working product in short cycles reduces time to market and helps stay ahead of the competition.
  - Better Management of Risks and Priorities: Identifying and managing risks earlier, prioritizing work based on value and urgency to keep the project on track.

  - Cost Control: Controls project costs by delivering valuable features first, avoiding waste, and ensuring every dollar spent moves closer to the goal.
- Overall, adopting Scrum can transform project management and product development by optimizing processes, aligning teams, satisfying customers, and delivering tangible value consistently.
- Whether you are a startup or an enterprise, considering Scrum as a project management approach can bring numerous advantages and enhance your chances of success in a competitive market.

- So, why not give it a try? The benefits observed from adopting Scrum are undoubtedly valuable.

3.1: Overview of the Scrum Lifecycle

Understanding the iterative and incremental approach of Scrum.Scrum Lifecycle: A Practical Overview

In the realm of project management, Scrum is akin to a finely tuned orchestra, where each element plays a pivotal role in creating harmony. At its core, Scrum revolves around an iterative and incremental approach, ensuring projects remain flexible and responsive to change. Let's break down the key components and roles that make this possible.

The Framework Essentials

Product Backlog: This is the master list of everything that needs to be done within the project, curated and prioritised by the product owner and defined as a list of user stories. Think of it as the project's wishlist, containing new features, enhancements, fixes, and everything in between. It's dynamic, constantly evolving based on the project's needs, stakeholder feedback, and market changes.

Sprint Backlog

Selected from the Product Backlog, this is the set of items the team commits to delivering in the upcoming sprint. It's essentially the team's to-do list for the sprint, carefully chosen and refined during the sprint planning meeting.

Sprint Planning

The kickoff for each sprint begins with this planning session. Here, the product owner outlines the highest priority items from the product backlog and, together with the team, decides what can be completed in the next sprint. This meeting sets the stage for the Sprint's objectives. Note how this planning has evolved over time. The requirements are still defined in User Stories (an account of a user's journey through a specific part of the system), but the way we size/estimate the implementation of those stories has evolved. We'll discuss defining and planning user stories in the artefacts and planning lessons later in the course.

The Sprint

A sprint is a time-boxed period, usually two to four weeks, where the selected work is developed and prepared for review. It's during this phase that user stories are transformed into tangible increments of the product.

Daily Scrum

A brief, daily meeting where the team syncs up on their progress, outlines their plans for the day, and discusses any impediments they might be facing. The Scrum Master facilitates these meetings to ensure the team remains on track and any blockers are addressed promptly.

Sprint Review

At the end of the sprint, the team demonstrates what they've completed during the sprint review meeting. It's a chance for stakeholders to see the progress, provide feedback, and adjust the product backlog as necessary.

Sprint Retrospective

Following the review, the team holds a retrospective to reflect on the past sprint. They discuss what went well, what didn't, and how they can improve in the next Sprint. This meeting is a key part of Scrum's continuous improvement ethos. You might have heard this meeting described as the "GBU" or "The Good, the Bad and the Ugly" meeting, although "retrospective" is the term currently most commonly used.

Roles That Make the World Go Round

Scrum Master: This role acts as the team's coach and protector.

The Scrum Master works to remove any impediments that are hindering the team's progress, facilitates Scrum events, and ensures the principles and practices of Scrum are followed. They also act as a buffer between the team and the outside world, deflecting external distractions and predatory approaches from other teams.

Product Owner: The visionary and voice of the customer.

The product owner is responsible for defining the product vision, ensuring the product backlog is up-to-date, and prioritising the work based on value to the business and customer.

The Scrum Team

A cross-functional group of professionals who work collaboratively to deliver the Sprint's goals. They are self-organizing, meaning they decide together how to get the work done, and are fully responsible for delivering high-quality increments. Cross-functional merely points to the fact that the team contains a number of different skill sets. For example, a typical Scrum team (release train in SAFe) probably contains a business analyst, a tester or test analyst,a couple of developers, an SME (subject matter expert), and possibly a technical architect and data analyst, depending on the team's focus.

The Iterative Beat Goes On

With each Sprint, the team builds, reviews, and adjusts, creating a rhythm that melds flexibility with productivity. The iterative approach ensures that feedback is rapidly incorporated and that the product evolves in a direction that meets user needs and business goals.

So, what should I expect on my first Scrum project?

A certain amount of pre-work should have been completed. The requirements should be complete. If you're starting a project, then you should know what it is that you want to build. When I say the requirements are complete, I'm not saying they can't be added to, just that there should be enough to get on with. The product backlog should exist, and the user's stories and features should be prioritised. Enough stories should have been moved to the top of the backlog to get the team through the first couple of sprints. I'm also assuming that DevOps should be in place and developer workstations and tools should be available to the team. Test teams should be available to support the user stories acceptance process.

Each Iteration(sprint) should look like this :

Step 1: sprint planning.

The team picks stories from the top of the backlog to work on during the sprint. These are moved to the sprint backlog. The team only moves as much work as it can realistically complete during the sprint, and commits to completing it.

Step 2 Development.

The team starts developing stories that have been committed to the sprint. During this time, the team should work only on the committed stories. How they do that is down the team. Scrum is a project management framework. However, there are Agile development approaches (things like BDD TDD or XP) that you can use in conjunction with Scrum to deliver the product. Some are frameworks in their own right; others are stand-alone agile practices. These can change over time and go in and out of fashion with changes in development technologies, so it's important to understand that a framework or approach is providing to make good choices in this area.

In Step 3, Sprint review

The completed features are demonstrated to the product owner, sponsors and team, including the Scrum Master.

Step 4 The sprint retrospective (GBU) takes place

, and required improvements are noted and implemented by the team.

In step 5,

the product owner validates the priority in the product backlog, and we go back to step 1.

A Practical Takeaway

Understanding the Scrum lifecycle from a practical perspective highlights its strengths in fostering adaptability, ensuring stakeholder engagement, and promoting continuous improvement. By appreciating the roles of the Scrum Master, Product Owner, and Scrum Team, along with the significance of the product and sprint backlogs, one can see how Scrum is designed to navigate the complexities of modern project management efficiently.

In essence, adopting Scrum is about embracing a mindset of collaboration, flexibility, and a relentless pursuit of value and quality. Whether you're embarking on a new project or seeking to improve your current processes, the Scrum lifecycle offers a roadmap for navigating the challenges with agility and confidence.

Recap

The Scrum Lifecycle is a project management framework emphasizing iterative and incremental approaches for flexibility and responsiveness to change. Key components and roles include:

- Product Backlog
- Sprint Backlog
- Sprint Planning
- Sprint Review
- Sprint Retrospective
- Scrum Master
- Product Owner
- Scrum Team

The Scrum process involves:

- Planning
- Development
- Review
- Retrospective sessions within time-boxed iterations known as sprints.

Benefits of Scrum and Agile development include:

- Adaptability
- Stakeholder engagement
- Continuous improvement

Embracing Scrum involves:

- Collaboration
- Flexibility
- Commitment to value and quality in project management

The Scrum project management framework offers:
Navigating project challenges with agility and confidence
The text explains:

- Steps in the Scrum lifecycle like working on committed stories, Sprint reviews, Sprint retrospectives, and validating priorities in the product backlog.
- Importance of understanding various frameworks and agile practices to make informed choices.

Emphasize the benefits of adopting Scrum:
- Fostering adaptability
- Stakeholder engagement
- Continuous improvement in project management

3.2: From Concept to Completion

Detailed walkthrough of the Scrum phases, including pre-sprint activities, sprint cycles, and post-sprint reviews.

So, before we get into the details of each Scrum Ceremony and Artefact, we thought it would be good to pull the camera back and look at the context from which a Scrum project is run. In the previous section, we discussed the Scrum lifecycle itself. In this section, we will discuss the things that sit outside and around the main Scrum and their interaction with it.

In the rapidly evolving landscape of project management, Scrum stands out as a highly effective agile framework, particularly suited for projects with complex deliverables, where requirements fluctuate and the path to the goal requires flexibility. This detailed walkthrough of the Scrum phases, from the preliminary stages through the sprint cycles to the concluding post-sprint reviews, will elucidate the systematic approach that underpins this methodology. The discussion will cover pre-sprint activities, the intricacies of sprint cycles, and the critical post-sprint reviews, providing a comprehensive overview of the process from concept to completion.

MCAREL Consulting
Superior Advisory Services for Gu dew to Custo ners

Pre-Sprint Activities

Conceptualisation and Initialisation

So before we even decide we want to use Scrum, the journey begins with an idea or a need. The initial phase involves defining the project's vision, which provides a strategic direction and sets the stage for the following detailed planning. Stakeholders, including the Product Owner, Scrum Master, and potential team members, collaborate to outline the project's objectives, scope, and potential constraints. This phase is critical for aligning expectations and ensuring a shared understanding of the project's goals. Throughout my career, I've heard this part of the project, also called 'Inception'. This phase involved documenting the requirements and creating user stories from them. When I worked on large-scale enterprise projects, configuring vertical software packages for the insurance industry. We worked with pre-built software packages, which we then configured to meet the customer's specific requirements. We had a set of processes and user stories, and customers would choose the ones they wanted to implement. Two things stand out about this type of project:

Firstly, detailed estimates and a release plan were required as part of the engagement with the customer.

Secondly, historically, we have had many projects, and with those came a lot of empirical data to support the estimation process.

Within the Agile community, there's the concept of no estimates, which finds this sort of detailed up-front estimations counterproductive. (There are detailed justifications for this position, which we'll go into later in the book.) Whether you choose to do a detailed up-front estimation will depend on the situation you find yourself in. If the engagement requires detailed estimates and you have a lot of good empirical data from previous projects, including experienced-based data. Then, you might lean towards a comprehensive estimate.

MCAREL Consulting
Superior Advisory services for Gu dew ro Custo men

If there is no contractual obligation to provide it and a lack of data to support the estimate, then you would probably do better leaning towards the no-estimates approach.

SAFe (Scaled Agile Framework) requires that a project scope be set up front, the work split into Program Increments(PIs) (my experience is that these consist of release cycles that contain multiple sprints running from three to six months), and a PI Planning phase where all of the next PI's work is estimated. Projects with a contractual requirement to provide long-term estimates in an Agile way, such as very large product developments, may well consider using SAFe to achieve this.

The Product Backlog

Once the vision is clear, the next step is to develop the Product Backlog, an ordered list of everything that might be needed in the product. The product backlog is the sole source of requirements for the product. The Product Owner is responsible for the backlog, including its content, availability, and prioritisation. Initially, the Product Backlog is populated with a broad list of requirements, which are progressively refined and detailed as the project evolves. A product backlog consists of a set of User Stories (or just stories) that detail pieces of functionality in the system. How you organise your stories can be very important to the outcome of the product. Large long-tail stories are called "Epics" and are usually split into constituent stories. For example, an online process for collecting payment in an online shop will consist of the capability to capture payment methods, retrieve payment methods, verify payment methods against the bank or payment gateway, submit the transaction and display the outcome to the customer. Each sub-story belongs to the same Epic, and most Agile project management software can link stories back to an Epic. Prioritisation of the backlog is how we decide what is going into the next Sprint. However, that prioritisation should also take account of the Epic hierarchy and dependencies between stories.

For example, an online process for collecting payment in an online shop will consist of the capability to capture payment methods, retrieve payment methods, verify payment methods against the bank or payment gateway, submit the transaction and display the outcome to the customer. Each sub-story belongs to the same Epic, and most Agile project management software can link stories back to an Epic. Prioritisation of the backlog is how we decide what is going into the next Sprint. However, that prioritisation should also take account of the Epic hierarchy and dependencies between stories.

Sprint Planning

Pre-sprint activities culminate in Sprint Planning. This session is facilitated by the Scrum Master and involves the entire Scrum Team. The primary objective is to decide on the work to be performed during the upcoming Sprint. The Product Owner presents the top items on the Product Backlog, and the team collectively decides how many of these items they can commit to delivering by the end of the Sprint. By the conclusion of Sprint Planning, the team has a Sprint Goal and a detailed plan for reaching it, encapsulated in the Sprint Backlog.

Sprint Cycles

Execution and Daily Stand-ups

A Sprint is a time-boxed period (usually 2-4 weeks) during which a usable and potentially releasable product increment is created. Sprints are at the heart of the Scrum process, with each cycle beginning immediately after the conclusion of the previous one. Daily Stand-up meetings, also known as Daily Scrums, facilitate quick information exchange. Team members discuss what they did the previous day, what they will do today, and any impediments they face, enabling swift resolution of blockers and maintaining momentum.

Continuous Collaboration

Collaboration doesn't stop at the Daily Stand-up. The Scrum Team engages in constant communication, fostering an environment of transparency and collective responsibility. This ongoing collaboration is vital for adapting to changes in project requirements or scope and for integrating stakeholder feedback into the development process. Traditionally, this aspect of Scrum has called for Co-located teams; we believe this is still the best way to organise organic collaboration within the team. However, events in the last few years have led to remote working for many teams. Teams have been forced to use technology to collaborate.
The technologies include cloud-hosted virtual workstations, cloud-based dev-ops, project management, continuous integration tools, and source control. Online meeting solutions like Zoom, MS Teams and Slack have also been very important.

Sprint Review and Retrospective

At the end of the Sprint, the team conducts a Sprint Review, inviting stakeholders to assess the increment produced. This is an opportunity for the Product Owner to gather feedback and adjust the Product Backlog if necessary. Following the review, the team will hold a Sprint Retrospective. This is a critical reflection session for the team to discuss what went well, what didn't, and how processes could be improved for the next Sprint.

Post-Sprint Reviews

Reflection and Adaptation

Post-sprint activities are pivotal for the iterative improvement and success of the Scrum process. The insights gained during the Sprint Retrospective are used to refine methodologies, improve efficiencies, and enhance team dynamics. This cycle of reflection and adaptation ensures that the Scrum framework remains responsive to the needs of the project, the team, and the stakeholders.

Backlog Refinement

After the Retrospective, the Product Owner refines the Product Backlog with input from the business stakeholders. This involves re-prioritising items based on feedback from the Sprint Review, updating the backlog to reflect any new requirements or changes, and removing tasks that are no longer necessary. This continuous refinement ensures that the backlog remains a relevant and accurate guide for the project's direction.

Planning for the Next Sprint

The cycle begins anew with planning for the next Sprint, informed by the lessons learned and adjustments made during the post-sprint review phase. This iterative process allows for continuous improvement and adaptation, with each cycle moving the project closer to its final vision.

Conclusion

From the initial conceptualisation to the final product delivery, the Scrum framework provides a structured yet flexible approach to project management. Through the delineation of pre-sprint activities, the execution of sprint cycles, and the reflection of post-sprint reviews, Scrum facilitates a dynamic environment where collaboration, adaptation, and continuous improvement are paramount. This walkthrough illustrates not only the phases of the Scrum but also the context in which they exist.

MCAREL Consulting
Superior Advisory Services for Guidance to Customers

Recap

- The Scrum framework is detailed in the text, outlining the different phases involved:
  - It underscores the significance of pre-Sprint activities such as setting project vision, stakeholder collaboration, and backlog refinement.
  - Exploration of Sprint planning, execution, daily stand-ups, continuous collaboration, reviews, retrospectives, and post-Sprint tasks is provided.

- The nature of Scrum is iterative and adaptive, with continuous improvement and collaboration being central:

-
  - Key elements like Sprint Planning, Execution, Daily Stand-ups, Collaboration, Review, Retrospective, Post-Sprint Reviews, Backlog Refinement, and Planning for the Next Sprint are explained.
  - Teams in Scrum follow iterative processes, continuously planning, executing, reviewing, adapting, and refining to deliver usable product increments.
  - Emphasis is on collaboration, transparency, and continuous improvement, with each Sprint cycle contributing to project success and alignment with stakeholder needs.

4.1: Scrum Master
Role, responsibilities, and how a Scrum Master facilitates the team.

Alright, let's dive into the world of Agile and unwrap the essence of one of its pivotal roles: the Scrum Master. Now, imagine you're part of a rugby team (stay with me here), where your goal is to get the ball over the line. In this context, think of the Scrum Master as the coach who ensures that everyone plays by the rules, knows their position, and executes their plays flawlessly, all while overcoming the muddy patches and tackles that come your way. The world of software development, much like rugby, needs someone who's adept at facilitating, guiding, and, yes, occasionally pulling you out of the mud.

MCAREL Consulting
Superior Advisory Services for our clients customers

The Role of a Scrum Master

The Scrum Master, in essence, is the heartbeat of the Scrum team. They're not the team leader in a traditional sense but more of a coach and facilitator. Their primary goal isn't to assign tasks or give orders but to ensure the Scrum framework is followed, allowing the team to be as effective and efficient as possible. They're akin to a gardener, ensuring that the environment is just right for the plants (team members) to grow and thrive, removing weeds (blockers), and ensuring the soil is fertile (the team is well facilitated).

Responsibilities of a Scrum Master

The responsibilities of a Scrum Master can be vast, but let's focus on the crux of their role:

Facilitating Meetings.

This includes daily stand-ups, sprint planning, retrospectives, and reviews. They ensure these meetings are productive, stay on topic, and finish on time. Imagine the Scrum Master as the conductor of an orchestra, ensuring every section comes in at the right time to create a symphony.

Removing Blockers

Blockers or impediments can be anything from technical hurdles, lack of resources, to inter-personal conflicts. The Scrum Master works diligently to remove these, ensuring the team's pathway to achieving their sprint goals is clear. This might involve negotiating with other departments, sourcing new tools, or simply ensuring the team has the right environment to focus on their work. As if it wasn't clear, it's the Scrum Master's responsibility to remove your blocker.

If your laptop doesn't have the right software installed, it's the Scrum Masters job to tell you where to get it, or contact the desktop support people to get it installed; To make sure your user id is set-up and you have the permissions needed, to install or download what you need, and get someone else in the team to help you if all that fails. "Call support; you'll find the support number on the company intranet" is not good enough. The velocity of your team is going to depend on how quickly and effectively the Scrum Master sweeps away impediments so that you can concentrate on delivering your stories.

Coaching and Mentoring

They provide guidance to the team on Scrum practices and principles, ensuring that the team understands the 'why' behind what they are doing. It's about empowering the team to find solutions rather than providing them outright.

Shielding the Team

The Scrum Master protects the team from external interruptions and distractions, allowing them to focus on the task at hand. This might mean fending off additional requests from stakeholders or managing expectations. In addition it's important that the Scrum Master is in a position to manage requests for a team members time from other projects/departments. When the tech lead get's casual requests for support from his old boss. These should be passed through the Scrum Master who in the majority of situations will reject them.

Facilitating Communication

They Scrum Master should ensure there is open and effective communication both within the team and with external stakeholders. This helps in aligning expectations and ensuring that everyone is on the same page.

Ensuring Continuous Improvement

Through retrospectives and feedback, the Scrum Master encourages the team to reflect on their processes and find ways to improve. It's about encouraging a culture of relentless improvement, where every sprint is an opportunity to get better.

How a Scrum Master Facilitates the Team

A Scrum Master facilitates the team by being the oil in the machine, ensuring everything runs smoothly. They do this by:

Listening Actively

By understanding the team's challenges and needs by being an active listener. This helps in preempting issues before they become blockers.

Being adaptable

the ability to react appropriately to Scrum updates from team members. If a team member flags an issue, the Scrum Master assesses and acts swiftly to mitigate it, whether it's by reallocating resources, providing additional support, or reprioritizing tasks.

Fostering a Collaborative Environment

Encouraging team members to share their updates, challenges, and solutions. This not only promotes transparency but also collaboration, as team members can offer help to each other.

Maintaining a Positive Environment

Keeping morale high, especially when the team faces challenges. Celebrating small wins, encouraging team bonding, and ensuring a positive work culture are all key.
In closing, the role of a Scrum Master is multifaceted, challenging, yet immensely rewarding. They are the team's guardian, ensuring that the Scrum framework is not just followed but leveraged to its fullest potential. By removing blockers, reacting swiftly to team updates, and encouraging an environment of collaboration and relentless improvement, the Scrum Master plays a critical role in navigating the team towards their goals. So, the next time you see a Scrum Master in action, remember that they're not just facilitating meetings; they're ensuring the team's pathway to success is as smooth as possible.

It should be obvious by now that a Scrum Master should be a very capable and resourceful person; it doesn't hurt at all if they participate and have experience in at least one or two of the cross-functional roles found in the team in addition to the Agile management skills they bring to the piece. Obtaining Scrum Master certification is always worthwhile, but knowing the technology, having great interpersonal skills, and a network of useful contacts within the organisation is probably as important, if not more important, to be successful in the role.

Recap

4.1: Scrum Master - Role, responsibilities, and how a Scrum Master facilitates the team. Let's delve into the Agile world and uncover the essence of a crucial role: the Scrum Master. Imagine you're part of a rugby team where the Scrum Master plays the role of a coach, ensuring everyone follows the rules, knows their position, and executes flawlessly.

- The Role of a Scrum Master:
  - The Scrum Master is the heartbeat of the team, acting as a coach and facilitator, not a traditional team leader. Their goal is to ensure the Scrum framework is followed for maximum team effectiveness.
  - They are like a gardener, creating the right environment for team growth by removing blockers and fostering a fertile team atmosphere.

- Responsibilities of a Scrum Master:

-
  - Facilitating Meetings: Conducting meetings like stand-ups, planning, and retrospectives to ensure productivity and timeliness.
  - Removing Blockers: Diligently working to eliminate obstacles hindering the team's sprint goals.
  - Coaching and Mentoring: Guiding the team on Scrum principles and practices, empowering them to find solutions.
  - Shielding the Team: Protecting the team from external distractions and interruptions.

-
  - Facilitating Communication: Ensuring open and effective communication within and outside the team to align expectations.
  - Continuous Improvement: Encouraging a culture of relentless improvement through retrospectives.
- How a Scrum Master Facilitates the Team:
  - By actively listening, being adaptable to team updates, fostering collaboration, and maintaining a positive work environment.
  - They react swiftly to issues, celebrate wins, encourage bonding, and promote continuous enhancement.

4.2: Product Owner - Exploring the role of the Product Owner in defining the product vision and managing the product backlog.

The role of the Product Owner in Agile project management is both pivotal and multifaceted, serving as the linchpin that connects the client, stakeholders, and development team. Their primary responsibilities involve defining the product vision and managing the product backlog. These tasks are crucial for aligning the project's objectives with the needs of the users and ensuring the delivery of valuable and relevant product features.

MCAREL Consulting
Superior Advisory Services for business customers

Defining the Product Vision

The product vision is the cornerstone of any project, outlining the long-term goals of the product and setting a broad, strategic direction. It acts as a guiding star for the Agile team, ensuring that everyone is aligned towards a common goal. The Product Owner, therefore, plays a crucial role in crafting and communicating this vision.

The vision statement should be clear, concise, and inspiring. It must convey the purpose of the product, its primary users, and the key benefits it offers. Importantly, it should also be broad enough to allow for flexibility in how the team achieves the end goal, yet specific enough to provide direction.

For example, a Product Owner in a software development company might define the vision for a new mobile application as follows: "To provide busy professionals with an easy-to-use mobile application that simplifies their workflow and increases productivity, accessible anywhere at any time." This vision clearly states who the product is for (busy professionals), what the product will do (simplify workflows and increase productivity), and its unique selling point (accessibility).

By defining a compelling product vision, the Product Owner sets the stage for all the strategic decisions that follow. This vision helps to prioritise features, manage stakeholder expectations, and guide the development team during the project lifecycle.

Managing the Product Backlog

The product backlog is a dynamic, ordered list of everything that is thought to be required in the product. It is the Product Owner's responsibility to create, maintain, and prioritise this backlog, ensuring that it is transparent, visible, and understood by all members of the team.

Creation and refinement

The initial product backlog is created by the product Owner based on the product vision. It starts as a high-level wishlist and is continuously refined and detailed throughout the project. This involves writing user stories, which are descriptions of features from the perspective of the end user. These stories help the team understand what needs to be built and why.

Prioritisation

One of the most critical tasks for the Product Owner is the prioritisation of the backlog items. This process involves assessing the relative importance and urgency of each item based on the overall business objectives, the needs of the users, and input from stakeholders and the development team. The Product Owner must also consider the cost of implementing each feature against its perceived value. This is an ongoing activity and must be revisited regularly as new information becomes available, market conditions change, or feedback from users is received.

Clarification Specification

The product Owner must ensure that the backlog items are clearly understood by the development team. This involves specifying acceptance criteria for user stories, which define the conditions under which a user story is considered complete and provide a basis for test cases that prove the acceptance criteria have been met. The Product Owner must be available to clarify requirements and make decisions about the product details on a day-to-day basis, facilitating the development process and helping to prevent any delays.

Grooming Sessions

Backlog grooming, or refinement, sessions are regular meetings led by the Product Owner to review items on the backlog to ensure they are appropriately prioritised and detailed. During these sessions, stories can be re-estimated, split, or merged; acceptance criteria can be updated, and any ambiguities addressed. We'll talk about Story Slicing and Leveling in the Planning lesson.

Challenges and Strategies

Being a Product Owner comes with its challenges, primarily related to managing diverse stakeholder interests and maintaining a clear focus on the product vision amidst changing conditions.
To be effective, Product Owners need to employ various strategies:

Stakeholder Engagement

Regular communication and involvement of stakeholders are essential in order to gather their insights and ensure their expectations are aligned with the project's progress. On larger project this may involve the formation of a steering committee with representatives from senior management, business owners and IT.

Customer Feedback

Incorporating feedback from end-users early and often allows the Product Owner to make informed decisions about feature prioritisation and adjustments.

Continuous Learning

Product Owners must stay informed about market trends, competitor activities, and new technologies to keep the product relevant and competitive.

In conclusion, the role of the Product Owner is crucial for the success of an Agile project. They not only define the product vision and ensure that it aligns with the business goals and user needs but also manage the product backlog to facilitate the smooth execution of project tasks. Through effective backlog management, clear communication, and strategic foresight, the Product Owner ensures that the development team can deliver a product that meets or exceeds the expectations of stakeholders and users alike. This balancing act between strategic vision and tactical execution makes the Product Owner a key player in the Agile process.

Recap

The role of the Product Owner in Agile project management is pivotal, serving as the linchpin connecting the client, stakeholders, and development team. Their primary responsibilities involve:

- Defining the product vision
- Managing the product backlog

Defining the Product Vision: The product vision is essential as it outlines the long-term goals of the product and sets a strategic direction. The Product Owner is crucial in crafting and communicating this vision by ensuring it is clear, concise, and inspiring. The vision statement should convey the purpose of the product, its primary users, and key benefits. For example, a mobile application vision could focus on simplifying workflows for busy professionals.

Managing the Product Backlog: The product backlog is a dynamic list of product requirements, and it is the Product Owner's responsibility to:

- Create and refine the backlog based on the product vision
- Prioritize backlog items considering business objectives, user needs, and stakeholder input
- Clarify and specify backlog items to ensure they are understood by the development team
- Conduct grooming sessions to review and update backlog items regularly

Challenges and Strategies: Product Owners face challenges in managing stakeholder interests and staying focused on the product vision. Effective strategies include:

- Engaging stakeholders through regular communication
- Incorporating customer feedback for informed decisions
- Continuously learning about market trends and technologies

Summary: The Product Owner's role is critical for Agile project success, aligning product vision with business goals, managing the backlog, and ensuring clear communication. By balancing strategic vision and tactical execution, the Product Owner helps deliver a product meeting stakeholder and user expectations.

4.3: The Development Team

Characteristics of cross-functional development teams, their roles, and responsibilities.

In the context of Agile methodologies, the concept of a cross-functional development team is central to achieving swift and adaptive software development. This section delves into the characteristics of such teams, their roles, and responsibilities, providing insight into how they contribute to the Agile process.

Characteristics of Cross-Functional Development Teams

Cross-functional development teams are composed of professionals with varied expertise and skills necessary to complete a project from start to finish. These teams are characteristically diverse, encompassing a range of functional abilities that typically include, but are not limited to, planning, requirement analysis, coding, testing, and deployment.

Diversity of Skills

Each member brings a unique set of skills that complements the team, allowing for a more holistic approach to development. This diversity extends beyond technical skills to include problem-solving, critical thinking, and creative capabilities, enhancing the team's ability to address complex project challenges.

Self-Organisation

Unlike traditional hierarchical teams, cross-functional teams are largely self-organising. This means they are empowered to make decisions about how to best achieve their objectives, without needing constant direction from higher management. This autonomy encourages a greater sense of ownership and accountability among team members.

Flexibility

The varied skills within the team allow it to be highly adaptable, adjusting its focus and methods as project needs evolve. This flexibility is crucial in Agile environments, where requirements can change rapidly based on stakeholder feedback and market conditions.

Collaborative Nature

Effective cross-functional teams prioritise communication and collaboration. Regular interactions through meetings like daily stand-ups or sprint reviews ensure that all members are aligned and can discuss challenges and progress openly.

Roles within Cross-Functional Development Teams

The structure of cross-functional teams can vary, but typically includes roles such as:

Product Owner

The Product Owner is responsible for defining the vision of the product, managing the product backlog, and ensuring that the team delivers value to the business. They act as a bridge between the development team and stakeholders, conveying needs and priorities.

Scrum Master

The Scrum Master facilitates the Scrum process, helping the team adhere to Agile practices and principles. They are not a traditional manager but a coach and facilitator, assisting the team in removing impediments and fostering an environment conducive to high performance. Some agile practitioners use the term 'Servant Leader' to identify leaders that serve the team, by providing insight, removing blockers and facilitating collaboration.

Team Member

These are the individuals who carry out the development work. In a cross-functional team, these roles are not rigid but are fluid, with members often taking on multiple responsibilities or swapping roles as needed to meet the team's goals.

Responsibilities of Cross-Functional Development Teams

The responsibilities of cross-functional development teams are comprehensive and dynamic, adapting to the needs of the project and the organisation.

Delivering High Quaity Product

The primary responsibility is to deliver a product that meets or exceeds customer expectations. This involves not only the technical development of the product but also ensuring it is user-friendly, reliable, and meets the defined requirements.

Managing the Product Backlog

The team works closely with the Product Owner to refine and prioritise the backlog items. This ongoing task ensures that the team is always working on the most valuable tasks and that the product evolves in a manner that maximises business value.

Stakeholder Engagement

Regular communication with stakeholders is vital to ensure that the team is aligned with business goals and stakeholder expectations. This includes demonstrating increments of the product and gathering feedback to integrate into future development cycles. In many cases, the Product Owner acts as a conduit for the flow of information between the stakeholders and the team.

Continuous Improvement

Agile methodologies emphasise continuous improvement in processes and products. The team routinely reflects on its performance and processes to identify areas for improvement, often during retrospective meetings at the end of each sprint.
In the context of Agile methodologies, particularly within frameworks such as Scrum, the cross-functional development team plays a critical role. These teams are composed of individuals with varied skills necessary to deliver a complete product. After discussing the core roles within a Scrum team—Product Owner and Scrum Master—it is essential to explore the diverse skill sets represented within a typical cross-functional team.

Skill Sets in Cross-Functional Development Teams

So, above, we describe the function of the team, but what makes it cross-functional? A cross-functional team in an Agile environment typically includes a mix of technical and non-technical skills that work together to handle all aspects of a project from inception to delivery. Here are some of the key skill sets expected in such a team:

Developers

These are the programmers who write, debug, and maintain the software. They are skilled in one or more programming languages relevant to the project and are familiar with best practices in coding and system design.

UI/UX Designers

User Interface (UI) and User Experience (UX) Designers are crucial for ensuring the software is both aesthetically pleasing and user-friendly. They design the layout and interactive elements of the application, focusing on optimising the user experience.

Testers/QA Specialists

Quality Assurance (QA) Specialists or Testers are responsible for ensuring the software meets all requirements and is free of bugs. Their role involves designing and implementing testing plans, carrying out tests, and documenting the results.

Business Analysts

Business Analysts bridge the gap between IT and the business stakeholders. They are responsible for gathering requirements, defining user stories, and ensuring that the delivered software aligns with business needs.

DevOps Engineers

DevOps Engineers focus on the processes and tools needed to integrate and deploy the software efficiently. They support the development team by improving system reliability and speeding up deployment cycles, often working with automated build and test environments and providing core tools like source control and CI/CD servers.

System Architects

System Architects design the overall structure of the IT system, ensuring that it is robust, scalable, and efficient. They make high-level design choices and dictate technical standards, including coding standards, tools, and platforms.

Integrating Skills for Effective Collaboration

The integration of these diverse skills is what makes a development team truly cross-functional. Each member not only contributes their specific expertise but also collaborates with others to cover the full spectrum of the project requirements. This integrated approach ensures that:

Design and Development are Aligned

UI/UX Designers work closely with Developers to ensure that the application is both functional and user-friendly.

Quality is Built In

Testers are integrated into the development process from the start, which helps in identifying and fixing issues early in the lifecycle.

Business Needs are Met

Business Analysts continuously align the development work with business goals, refining requirements and prioritising tasks.

MCAREL Consulting
Superior Advisory Services for Business Customers

Deployment is Streamlined

DevOps Engineers automate and streamline deployment, which enhances the agility and responsiveness of the team.

By harnessing these varied skills, cross-functional teams can effectively address the complex challenges typical of modern software projects, delivering products that are not only technically sound but also closely aligned with user needs and business objectives. This holistic approach is fundamental to Agile practices, promoting adaptability, teamwork, and a continuous improvement ethos throughout the project lifecycle.

In conclusion, cross-functional development teams are pivotal in Agile projects, driving the development process through their diverse skills, collaborative nature, and flexible approach. Their roles and responsibilities are interdependent, requiring constant communication and adaptation to ensure successful project outcomes. As Agile methodologies continue to evolve, the effectiveness of these teams remains a cornerstone of Agile success, embodying the principles of iterative development and continuous improvement.

Recap

Cross-functional development teams play a crucial role in Agile projects by bringing together diverse skills to tackle complex challenges in modern software development:

- These teams integrate expertise in design, development, testing, business analysis, and DevOps.
- Collaboration among team members is essential, requiring constant communication and adaptation for successful project outcomes.
- The holistic approach of cross-functional teams promotes adaptability, teamwork, and continuous improvement throughout the project lifecycle.

The characteristics and importance of cross-functional development teams in Agile methodologies include:

- Composed of professionals with diverse expertise necessary for efficient project completion.
- Team members possess a variety of skills, are self-organizing, flexible, and prioritize collaboration.
- Key roles within these teams include Product Owner, Scrum Master, and Team Members, with responsibilities focusing on delivering high-quality products, managing the product backlog, stakeholder engagement, and continuous improvement.

The variety of skill sets required in cross-functional teams underscores the emphasis on collaboration and integration to effectively address complex project challenges. This approach highlights the importance of Agile principles, adaptability, teamwork, and continuous improvement in achieving successful project outcomes.

5.1: Sprint Planning – Objectives, participants, and the process of planning sprints.

Part 1: Preparation for Sprint Planning

Setting the Stage

Effective sprint planning is essential for a successful execution phase in Agile project management. This preparation ensures that all team members are on the same page regarding the goals and expectations of the upcoming sprint. The three key areas of focus for setting the stage are: reviewing the product vision and roadmap, confirming the availability of team members, and ensuring the technological setup is adequate, especially for virtual meetings.

Review of the Product Vision and Roadmap

Understanding the Big Picture

The first step in preparing for sprint planning is to revisit the product vision and roadmap. This is not merely about having a document that charts the course but understanding how the upcoming sprint will help achieve the broader goals set for the product. It's about ensuring that every task planned aligns with the strategic direction of the product or service being developed.

Engagement with Stakeholders

This review should involve key stakeholders, including the product owner, who possesses a deep understanding of the market, customer needs, and the strategic fit of the product. Engaging with these stakeholders ahead of the sprint planning helps clarify the priorities and refine the focus of the sprint, ensuring that it contributes effectively to the product's lifecycle.

Refining the Roadmap

The product roadmap may evolve based on feedback from previous sprints, changes in market conditions, or new strategic objectives. Therefore, updating and aligning the roadmap is crucial before the team commits to the work for the next sprint. This ensures that everyone is moving towards a common goal and that the efforts are not divergent from the intended product trajectory.

Availability of Team Members

Scheduling and Confirmations

A successful sprint planning session requires the presence of all core team members who will be involved in the sprint. This includes the Scrum Master, Product Owner, and all other team members who will contribute to the sprint. Confirming the availability of these key personnel is essential; their input, expertise, and consensus are vital for a productive planning meeting.

Accommodating Team Needs

When scheduling the sprint planning session, consider the personal and professional schedules of all participants. This may involve finding a common time slot that fits different time zones, especially for distributed teams. Early confirmation helps in addressing any potential scheduling conflicts and allows team members to prepare adequately for the meeting.

Flexibility and Contingency Planning

Sometimes, despite best efforts, not all participants can attend. In such cases, having a contingency plan is vital. This could involve rescheduling the meeting to accommodate essential members or arranging for remote participation via video conferencing tools.

Technological Setup

Ensuring Smooth Virtual Meetings

For teams that operate remotely, the technological setup is a critical component of sprint planning preparation. This involves more than just having a functional video conferencing tool; it includes testing all equipment, ensuring stable internet connectivity, and having backups in place to handle any technical glitches.

Pre-Meeting Tech Check

Conduct a technical rehearsal before the meeting. This should include testing the video and audio clarity, sharing screens to ensure all participants can view presentations or documents, and verifying that all collaboration tools are operational. This check should ideally be done a day or two in advance to allow time for resolving any issues.

Training and Familiarisation

All team members should be comfortable using the chosen technological tools and platforms. If new tools or updates have been introduced since the last planning session, consider a quick training session or a guide to ensure everyone is on the same page. This prevents delays during the actual meeting and reduces the time spent troubleshooting basic issues.

Conclusion

The preparation phase of sprint planning is crucial for setting the stage for a focused and productive session. By carefully reviewing the product vision and roadmap, ensuring all key team members can attend, and preparing the technological setup, the team can enter the sprint planning session with clarity and readiness. This upfront investment in preparation significantly enhances the effectiveness of the sprint planning process, ultimately contributing to the successful delivery of project goals.

Part 2 : Techniques for Backlog Organisation

A good product backlog is a prerequisite for a successful sprint and a good sprint planning session. Backlog and story grooming are something that usually happens before we get to the Scrum part of the project. But as we are going to literally sprint through the work then the stories need to be in good condition before we start and we need to know our priorities.

Ever since I started using Agile methods on customer projects, I've used an estimation process for stories in the product backlog. Stories come into the backlog as raw requirements, good ideas, or even very detailed designed processes. We'd have Epic stories like "As a user, I need an online process to create an insurance quote for a commercial property insurance policy." This one is going to take a couple of sprints to complete. Then you might have a story like, "As the first part of the quote wizard, I need a screen to collect contact details and verify them against our CRM system." This one may take a whole sprint to complete or maybe more, as it can't be categorised as complete until both the screen and the integration with CRM have been completed.

In both examples, the stories need to be split or "sliced" into a set of new stories, each of which can be completed within a sprint and developed in parallel. Then you will have stories like "As a Customer service representative creating an insurance quote, I need a screen at the beginning of the flow to capture contact details." and "As a Customer Service Representative, I need to verify the contact details I've collected in the quote flow against CRM". The first story covers the UI part of the data collection and display. The second story is an integration story where the contact data is sent to CRM for verification. These probably don't need to be split any further.

In the next couple of paragraphs, we'll discuss some of the techniques traditionally used to groom or organise the product backlog for sprint planning. Some are now considered old-fashioned and obsolete, but they are included because you may be using them already or may have encountered them in your background reading. Others are bang up to date (for now).

When choosing an approach, the following sometimes contradictory aims are important
:

- Take account of dependencies by slicing vertically - Your objective is to deliver a working piece of business capability to the customer as you deliver each story. If, as in the example above, you deliver the screen without the CRM integration, then the screen is not usable. This may be unavoidable in some situations(the integration is not so straightforward). But, where possible, deliver stories vertically, providing functionality that works top to bottom.

- Manage the size of your stories so they can be completed in a sprint: The smaller and more detailed they are, the easier they are to implement, and the easier it is for the Scrum Master to track your progress throughout the sprint.
- Predictability of outcomes: smaller stories are easier to size and move around within the backlog. If all your stories take a sprint to complete, then it's harder to pull new work into the sprint if you finish early.

Story Leveling

Understanding Story Leveling
Story Leveling involves categorising user stories into groups based on their perceived complexity and effort. This technique helps the team manage and prioritise work more effectively by aligning tasks that require similar levels and types of resources.
Implementation of Story Leveling

1. Grouping Stories: Begin by categorising stories into 'simple', 'moderate', and 'complex'. Each category reflects a range of complexity and effort needed.
2. Criteria Setting: Define clear criteria for each category. For instance, simple tasks might require minimal dependencies and effort, while complex tasks could involve multiple team members and significant uncertainty.
3. Review and Adjust: Continuously review and adjust the levelling as more information becomes available or the project evolves.
4. Split stories: split into multiple smaller stories and group them into epics to manage dependencies between them.

Benefits of Story Leveling

- Enhanced Focus: Teams can focus on completing groups of stories that are at a similar level of difficulty.
- Improved Prioritisation: It is easier to prioritise tasks within the same complexity level.
- Better Resource Allocation: Enables more strategic allocation of resources across the team.

Planning Poker

Introduction to Planning Poker

Planning Poker, or Scrum Poker, is a fun, consensus-based technique for estimating the size of user stories in terms of story points. It involves all team members, making it a collaborative process.

How to Play Planning Poker

1. Card Distribution: Each participant receives a deck of cards, each card representing a different number of story points (usually a Fibonacci sequence like 1, 2, 3, 5, 8, 13, etc.).
2. Presentation of User Stories: The product owner or facilitator presents a user story to the team.
3. Private Estimation: Each team member selects a card that they believe reflects the complexity and effort required for the story.
4. Reveal and Discuss: All cards are revealed simultaneously. If estimates differ significantly, team members discuss their reasoning and re-estimate until a consensus is reached.

Advantages of Planning Poker

- Encourages Team Collaboration: Involves the entire team in the estimation process.
- Provides Multiple Perspectives: Helps surface different perspectives on the effort required, leading to more accurate estimates.
- Reduces Anchoring Bias: Prevents team members from being influenced by others' estimates before revealing their own.

Estimating with Story Points

Concept of Story Points

Estimating with Story Points involves assigning a numerical value to each user story to represent its relative effort, complexity, and risk. This abstract metric helps teams compare tasks without getting tied to specific time estimates, which can vary widely among individuals.

How to Implement Story Points

1. Define Scale: Establish a baseline story (often something small and well-understood) and assign it a value (e.g., one story point). Other stories are estimated relative to this baseline.
2. Estimate as a Team: The entire team engages in estimating stories, ensuring a broad perspective on the effort required.
3. Use Historical Data: Over time, collect data on story points and actual effort required to refine future estimations.

Benefits of Using Story Points

- Focus on Value Over Time: Encourages the team to think about value delivered rather than time spent.
- Accommodates Uncertainty: Allows for uncertainty in estimating tasks that have unclear requirements.
- Facilitates Better Sprint Planning: Helps in planning sprints more accurately based on team velocity.

Note estimating with story points is considered(in some circles) an outdated approach. But it has been ubiquitous for a number of years previously. If you've worked on Agile projects in the past then you'll have probably come across this approach in practice. And of course, if you're doing some background reading, you'll probably come across it there as well. Story points can work very well where the stories are estimated in points (using a nominal hour value for a point) and the delivery is measured in hours. You can then use the points and hours burned to calculate how many hours a point actually resolves to.

Story Slicing

Breaking Down Complex Stories

Story Slicing involves breaking down user stories into smaller, more manageable components that can realistically be completed within a sprint. This technique is particularly useful for large or complex stories that could potentially monopolise team resources.

Steps for Effective Story Slicing

1. Identify Large Stories: Start by identifying stories that seem too large to be completed comfortably in a single sprint.
2. Divide into Smaller Tasks: Break these stories into smaller tasks that each deliver value and are independently testable. Stories should be sliced vertically to manage dependencies. Schemes exist with multiple complex slicing critieria.
3. Ensure Manageability: Each sliced story should be manageable and understandable, with clear acceptance criteria.

Advantages of Story Slicing

- Increases Flexibility: Smaller stories can be more easily moved around in the sprint for better flexibility.
- Improves Understanding: Helps the team understand and execute each part of the story better.
- Enhances Predictability: Smaller tasks are easier to estimate and thus enhance the predictability of sprint outcomes.

Slicing is a topic all of it's own and sits outside the scope of this book. You'll find references at the end of the course.

Conclusion

Incorporating these backlog estimation techniques into your Agile practice can significantly enhance the planning and execution of sprints. Whether it's grouping tasks by complexity with Story Leveling, engaging in a collaborative game of Planning Poker, assigning abstract Story Points, or breaking down tasks with Story Slicing, each method offers unique benefits. By understanding and applying these techniques, teams can achieve more accurate estimations, better resource management, and ultimately, more successful project deliveries.

Part 3: Sprint planning the meeting itself.

Introduction

So, to recap, we've discussed preparation for the Sprint planning meeting. We've talked about some of the approaches used historically to categorise/estimate the user stories and size stories so they can be completed within the sprint. Now, we'll go through the meeting itself.

Objectives of Sprint Planning

The primary objectives of sprint planning include:

1. Defining the Sprint Goal: The sprint goal is a short, concise statement that outlines what the team aims to achieve during the sprint. This goal guides the team's work throughout the sprint, providing a focus and fostering cohesion.

2. Selecting Items from the Product Backlog: The team chooses which items from the product backlog they will work on during the sprint, ensuring these items align with the sprint goal and are feasible within the sprint's timeframe.

3. Formulating a Plan for Deliverables: The team plans how to turn the backlog items into a working increment. This involves discussions on the approach, division of tasks, and identification of potential challenges.

Participants in Sprint Planning

The success of sprint planning depends heavily on the active participation of the following roles:

- Product Owner: Responsible for representing the interests of the stakeholders and the voice of the customer. The product owner prioritises the backlog items and clarifies the acceptance criteria for the backlog items during the planning.

- Development Team: Consists of the professionals who do the work of delivering the product increment. They are responsible for estimating the effort required and determining the number of items they can commit to during the sprint.

- Scrum Master: Acts as a facilitator for the sprint planning meeting. The Scrum Master ensures that the meeting is productive and that the team adheres to the time constraints and Scrum principles.

The Process of Sprint Planning

Sprint planning is typically divided into two parts: What and How.

Part 1: What

1. Product Owner Presents the Backlog: The product owner starts by presenting the prioritised product backlog items outlining the business objectives. This helps the team understand the background and the importance of each item.
2. Team Selects the Work: The development team then discusses the items, asks questions for clarity and assesses their complexity and effort. The team selects the items they can realistically complete during the sprint based on their capacity.
3. Setting the Sprint Goal: The team collaborates to define a sprint goal that aligns with the selected backlog items. This goal should be specific, measurable, achievable, relevant, and time-bound (SMART).

Part 2: How

1. Task Breakdown: The selected stories are broken down into smaller, manageable tasks. This is often done through story slicing, where each backlog item is dissected into more detailed user stories if necessary. Note this process may have been initiated during backlog grooming prior to the planning meeting. However, at this point in the meeting we may start to factor in more technical considerations from the development team.
2. Effort Estimation: Each user story is estimated using appropriate techniques, such as Planning Poker, to ensure a realistic understanding of the workload. This helps the team commit to the work without overburdening themselves.

MCAREL Consulting
Superior Advisory Services for Guidance to Customers

3. Resource Allocation: The team discusses the allocation of resources, including personnel and any external dependencies that could impact the sprint.
4. Risk Assessment: Identifying potential risks and discussing mitigation strategies is crucial to ensure smooth progress throughout the sprint.
5. Final Commitment: The team reviews the plan and makes a final commitment to the sprint goal. This commitment is an agreement among the team members about what they believe they can deliver. The commitment is to meeting the sprint goals. Adjustments may be made to the stories included in the delivery to meet those goals.

Conclusion

Sprint planning is not just about selecting tasks; it's about setting a realistic and achievable course for the sprint. It involves collaboration, transparency, and a clear understanding of the team's capacity and the project's requirements.

By the end of this session, the team should have a sprint backlog that outlines the work to be done, a clear sprint goal that guides the team's efforts, and a plan that details how the work will be achieved. This ensures everyone is aligned and has a shared understanding of the path forward.

Reflection

To reinforce your understanding, consider how sprint planning might differ in a team where the product owner is not very engaged versus a team with a highly proactive product owner. What challenges might arise, and how could the team adapt their approach to planning?

This section on sprint planning is crucial for anyone involved in Agile projects, as it lays the foundation for a successful sprint, ensuring that the team is prepared and fully aligned with the project's goals.

Recap

The importance of sprint planning in Agile projects is crucial to ensure team preparedness and alignment with project goals. The level of engagement of the product owner greatly influences sprint planning effectiveness, requiring teams to adapt planning approaches accordingly. Key elements of effective sprint planning highlighted in the text are:

- Story points
- Story slicing
- Story leveling
- Planning poker
- Estimating with story points

These techniques aid in breaking down complex user stories into manageable tasks for completion within a sprint. By incorporating these methods, teams can enhance resource management, predict sprint outcomes better, and achieve successful project deliveries. Sprint planning meetings hold significant importance in defining sprint goals, selecting backlog items, formulating deliverables, and ensuring active involvement of key roles such as the product owner, development team, and Scrum Master. The process involves determining "What" needs to be done and deciding "How" to achieve it collaboratively, promoting transparency...

Key takeaways from Lesson 1 on effective Sprint Planning in Agile project management include the need for clear goals and expectations among team members. Important preparation steps encompass reviewing the product vision, confirming team availability, ensuring technological readiness, stakeholder engagement, refining the product roadmap, and preparing for virtual meetings. Lesson 2 delves into techniques for organizing the product backlog, stressing the significance of a well-prepared backlog for successful sprints and planning sessions:

- Story grooming
- Estimation processes for stories
- Story leveling
- Planning poker for estimating story points collaboratively

Managing story dependencies, sizing stories appropriately for sprints, grouping stories by complexity, and using story points for relative estimation aid in prioritizing work effectively, resource management, and accurate sprint planning.

This lesson on preparing for Sprint Planning in agile project management focuses on setting the stage effectively by reviewing the product vision and roadmap, confirming team availability, and ensuring technological setup for virtual meetings. Key points covered include:

- Reviewing product vision and roadmap
- Confirming team availability
- Ensuring proper technological setup for virtual meetings
- Engaging with stakeholders prior to Sprint Planning
- Refining the product roadmap and accommodating team needs

Techniques for backlog organization such as story grooming, story leveling, planning poker, and estimating with story points are discussed to effectively manage and prioritize work. The concepts of story points, story slicing, story leveling, planning poker, and sprint planning meetings are covered. Key techniques explained include:

- Assigning story points to represent relative effort
- Breaking down complex stories through story slicing
- Categorizing user stories based on complexity with story leveling
- Collaborative estimating with planning poker

Sprint planning involves defining goals, selecting backlog items, formulating deliverables, and involves active participation from roles like product owner, development team, and Scrum Master. The process includes determining WHAT and HOW:

- WHAT: Prioritizing backlog items and setting sprint goals
- HOW: Task breakdown, effort estimation, resource allocation, risk assessment, and final commitment to sprint goals

Incorporating these techniques into Agile practices enhances planning and execution in sprints, providing more accurate estimations, better resource management, and successful project deliveries. Sprint planning is crucial in Agile projects to ensure team alignment and preparedness. Effective sprint planning involves clear goals, preparation steps, backlog organization techniques, and collaborative estimation processes for successful project deliveries.

5.2 Daily Scrum: Purpose and Conduct of Daily Stand-Up Meetings

The Daily Scrum, often referred to as the daily stand-up, is a fundamental component of the Scrum framework used in agile project management, particularly in software development. This brief, time-boxed meeting fosters communication, enhances team collaboration, and promotes quick decision-making within agile teams. This section explores the purpose, structure, and conduct of daily scrum meetings, providing a comprehensive guide for teams aiming to optimise their daily interactions.

Purpose of the Daily Scrum

The primary purpose of the Daily Scrum is to synchronise activities and create a plan for the next 24 hours. This meeting helps the team to align their work and progress towards the sprint goals. It is designed to inform all team members about where the project stands and to identify any potential roadblocks that could impede progress. Here are the key objectives:

Transparency

Ensuring that every team member is aware of the project's progress and any issues their teammates are facing.

Inspection

Team members reflect on their progress towards the sprint goal and adapt their next steps accordingly.

Adaption

The meeting enables the team to discuss challenges and collaboratively decide on necessary adjustments to their work or strategy.

Participants

The Daily Scrum is intended for the development team. The Scrum Master facilitates the session to ensure it runs smoothly and remains within the time limit. Although the Product Owner is not required to attend, their participation can be beneficial, particularly when clarification regarding the product backlog or priority features is needed.

Timing and Duration

The Daily Scrum is held every working day of the sprint at the same time and place to reduce complexity and increase routine. The recommended duration is strictly 15 minutes, which encourages conciseness and focus. Starting the day with the Daily Scrum can help set the tone for a productive day.

Structure and Conduct

Setting the Agenda

Although informal, the structure of the Daily Scrum is crucial for its effectiveness. The meeting typically revolves around three key questions that each team member answers:
1. What did I accomplish yesterday?
2. What will I do today?
3. What obstacles are impeding my progress?
These questions focus the discussion on progress and immediate plans, facilitating a rapid exchange of information among team members.

Conducting the Meeting

The Daily Scrum should be a dynamic and engaging interaction among team members, rather than a status update to the Scrum Master or Product Owner. To maintain energy and focus, many teams conduct the meeting standing up, which encourages brevity and active participation.

Role of the Scrum Master

The Scrum Master plays a key role in facilitating the Daily Scrum. They are responsible for ensuring that the meeting adheres to its time frame and that it remains focused on the agenda. The Scrum Master also helps the team in addressing impediments and ensuring that solutions are actively pursued after the meeting.

Engagement and Interaction

The Daily Scrum is not just about reporting statuses but also about team interaction and problem-solving. Team members should be encouraged to interact directly, offer help, suggest solutions, and coordinate their work beyond just answering the three questions.

Common Challenges and Solutions

Monotony and Disengagement

Repetitive sessions can lead to disengagement. To counteract this, teams can occasionally change the format slightly, such as walking meetings, or have different team members facilitate the meeting.

Time Management

Straying off-topic can extend the duration and dilute the focus of the meeting. The Scrum Master should gently steer the conversation back on track when necessary and handle discussions that require more time outside of the Daily Scrum.

Problem-Solving in the Meeting

While it is important to identify impediments during the Daily Scrum, detailed problem-solving should be reserved for a separate session. This ensures that the stand-up remains brief and focused.

Example Daily Updates

So, as mentioned above, the structure of your update should be in the form :

Last 24 I worked on x

Next 24 I plan to work on Y

I have a blocker - <describe blocker>:no blockers

But how you deliver the update can have a big impact on how useful it is to the team and scrum master.

Example 1: The no useful info update.

Last 24: Coding

Next 24: Coding

Blockers: None

Updates like this don't really let people know what you're working on, what you plan to work on tomorrow, or if there's anything they can help you with. Updates like this can indicate that you're struggling but are reluctant to let the team know, especially if you're giving this update for a number of days in a row.

Example 2: The overly detailed update

Last 24: List of classes you created, mini framework you created, details of your conversation with your SME. Details of a bug you found that's fixed now and how you fixed it etc.

Next 24: Detailed list of the things you plan on doing tomorrow, how long they're going to take. Say you need some input from the tech lead. Start a solution session in the meeting and spend the next 20 minutes debating with her, while everyone waits to give their update.

Blockers : I was blocked by a bug, but I fixed it, and now I'm free to continue.

Updates should concentrate on what you worked on and when you're likely to finish it. What you're planning to work on and how long you expect it to take. If you need a solution session, let the tech lead know you need to connect and schedule a meeting to cover that topic outside of the stand-up. Blockers should be current i.e. an issue that is currently stopping you moving forward.

Example 3: Good Update

Last 24: I continued coding for User Story 123456, and that's going well. I also reviewed Joe's pull request and merged it to develop.

Next 24: I intend to finish coding User Story 123456, complete unit testing and push my feature to the remote repo. I need to chat with Samira about an upcoming story 123457. Can we get together after this meeting?

Blocker: I need to integrate and test my code against a service provided by ACME Software Inc., but I don't have access to their test service.

So, points about this to update. The update includes the I.D. for the specific story being worked on. It includes an estimate of when the work will be completed. This way, the Scrum master can ensure that the developer is working on the correct story and making progress. The blocker is a current issue that needs attention. The Scrum Master can use the information to chase the vendor for the required access and assign the developer a new story to work on while he's waiting for the blocker to be resolved. The team member wants to meet with the tech lead, so he asks to meet her after the meeting. From the Scrum Masters' point of view, this update gives them good information. If they hear the same update 3 days running, they can begin to ask questions, "Are you stuck?", "Do you have a blocker?" "Have you been working on something else?". In this manner, issues can be detected and mitigated before they become serious problems.

Conclusion

The Daily Scrum is a vital tool in the agile toolkit, designed to enhance transparency, foster collaboration, and maintain momentum within the team. By adhering to the guidelines on structure and conduct, teams can maximise the effectiveness of their daily meetings, ensuring smooth progression towards their sprint goals and, ultimately, the successful delivery of the project. Effective Daily Scrums contribute significantly to the agile ethos of continuous improvement and responsiveness to change, underscoring their importance in the agile project management landscape.

Recap

The text emphasizes the importance of daily standup meetings in Agile methodology, highlighting the significance of addressing blockers that hinder progress. It stresses the need for team members to communicate issues promptly for swift resolution, promoting transparency and collaboration.

- Daily standup meetings aim to synchronize activities, enhance communication, and foster collaboration in Agile project management.
- Key objectives include transparency, inspection, and adaptation.
- Participants typically include the development team, with the Scrum Master facilitating the session.

It's recommended to strictly adhere to a 15-minute time limit for daily standups, focusing on three key questions to ensure a productive discussion. The Scrum Master's role is crucial in maintaining the agenda and addressing impediments effectively.

- Challenges like monotony, time management, and problem-solving are discussed with solutions provided.
- Effective delivery of updates by team members is essential, emphasizing providing relevant information and addressing blockers.

In conclusion, well-structured Daily Scrum meetings are fundamental in Agile project management, fostering transparency, collaboration, and continuous improvement. Following guidelines on structure and conduct can help teams optimize their interactions and progress towards project goals.

5.3: Sprint Review and Retrospective -

Explaining the significance of reviewing work and reflecting on the sprint process for continuous improvement.

Sprint Review and Retrospective are pivotal within the framework of Agile project management, particularly in Scrum methodology. These sessions focus on reviewing the work completed during the sprint and reflecting on the sprint process to enable continuous improvement. This discussion will elaborate on the significance of both practices and how they contribute to the evolving success of agile teams.

MCAREL Consulting
Superior Advisory services for Guidew to Customer

My Ebook

Sprint Review

The Sprint Review marks the culmination of the sprint and is a key event where the Scrum team and stakeholders convene to inspect the increment of the product that has been built during the sprint. The primary aim is to gather feedback to ensure that the product is developing in alignment with the user's needs and expectations.

Purpose and Benefits

Feedback on the Product Increments

The team presents the work they have completed, allowing stakeholders to interact with the new features. This immediate feedback is crucial as it influences future sprint planning, ensuring that the product evolves in a direction that delivers maximum value.

Collaboration and Communication

The review serves as a platform for direct communication between the team and the stakeholders. This interaction enhances understanding and alignment on the product vision and current market needs.

Transparency and Trust

By openly discussing the work completed, challenges faced, and work left undone, the team fosters transparency and builds trust with the stakeholders.

Conducting an Effective Sprint Review

Preparation: The team prepares a demo of the product increment to clearly show what has been accomplished. This involves ensuring that all functionalities are in a presentable state.

Inclusion of Stakeholders

It's important to include all relevant stakeholders in the review to gather diverse inputs and ensure the product is meeting broad expectations.

Focus on Outcomes

The discussion should focus on the product and its features rather than just the individual tasks or the process followed. The Product Owner should take notes on where the demonstrated product diverges from the stakeholder expectations. These notes should either be created as bugs for resolution or, if the issue highlights a difference in the required functionality then the required behavious should be added to the Product backlog and included in the upcoming sprint planning meeting.

My Ebook

Sprint Retrospective

Following the sprint review, the Sprint Retrospective offers the team an opportunity to look inward and evaluate their own processes, tools, and interactions. The retrospective is aimed at continuous process improvement, increasing efficiency and effectiveness in future sprints.

Purpose and Benefits

Identify Improvements

The retrospective helps the team identify what went well and what didn't, focusing on processes, tools, and interactions. This identification leads to actionable insights to implement in future sprints.

Team Building and Morale

Regular retrospectives help in building a stronger, more cohesive team as members openly discuss issues and achievements. This can significantly increase the teams' morale and motivation.

Adaptation and Flexibility

Continuous improvement is at the heart of Agile. By regularly adjusting their practices based on retrospective feedback, teams can become more adaptive and flexible, enhancing their ability to meet changing requirements.

Conducting an Effective Retrospective

Safe Environment

It is crucial to create an environment where team members feel safe to express their thoughts and feedback honestly without fear of blame.

Structured Format

Use formats such as "What went well?", "What could be improved?", and "What will we commit to improve in the next sprint?" to structure the discussion or indeed GBU.

Actionable Items

The team should leave the retrospective with concrete, actionable items that aim to address the discussed issues or reinforce positive practices.

Continuous Improvement

The practices of Sprint Review and Retrospective are fundamental in driving continuous improvement in Agile projects. The iterative nature of these meetings ensures that the product and the process evolve together towards excellence. Feedback from the review informs what should be built next, while insights from the retrospective refine how it should be built. This dual approach helps in maintaining a high level of performance and adaptability in the dynamic landscape of project development.

By diligently conducting these sessions and genuinely acting on the insights gathered, teams not only improve their workflows and outputs but also cultivate a culture of continuous learning and improvement. This culture is essential for sustaining innovation and excellence in an increasingly competitive and complex environment.

In conclusion, both the Sprint Review and Retrospective are indispensable for Agile teams aiming to deliver high-quality products that meet user needs while also refining their processes to be more efficient and effective. These practices not only ensure the product's alignment with the market but also enhance the team's capability to deliver with agility and quality.

Recap

Sprint Review and Retrospective are essential practices within the Agile project management framework, particularly in Scrum methodology. These sessions aim to review the work completed during a sprint and reflect on the sprint process for continuous improvement. Let's delve into the significance of both practices:

Sprint Review:

- The Sprint Review occurs at the end of a sprint, where the Scrum team and stakeholders gather to inspect the product increment developed during the sprint to ensure alignment with user needs.

MCAREL Consulting
Superior Advisory services for Gu dew re Custo ners

My Ebook

- Purpose and Benefits:
    - Feedback on the Product Increment: Stakeholders interact with new features, influencing future sprint planning for maximum value delivery.
    - Collaboration and Communication: Enhances alignment on the product vision and current market needs through direct interaction.
    - Transparency and Trust: Fosters trust with stakeholders by openly discussing completed work, challenges, and pending tasks.

Conducting an Effective Sprint Review:

- Preparation involves showcasing the product increment to stakeholders in a presentable state, ensuring all functionalities are demonstrated.
- Including all relevant stakeholders is crucial to gather diverse inputs and meet broad expectations.
- The focus of the discussion should be on the product's features rather than individual tasks or processes followed.

Sprint Retrospective:

- Following the Sprint Review, the Retrospective offers the team a chance to internally evaluate processes, tools, and interactions, aiming for continuous improvement in future sprints.
- Purpose and Benefits:
    - Identifying Improvements: Helps the team pinpoint successes and areas for improvement, leading to actionable insights for future sprints.
    - Team Building and Morale: Enhances team cohesion, morale, and motivation by openly discussing achievements and issues.

Conducting an Effective Retrospective:

- Create a safe environment for honest feedback without fear of blame.
- Use a structured format, such as discussing what went well, what could be improved, and commitments for the next sprint.
- Ensure actionable items are generated from the Retrospective to address issues or reinforce positive practices.

These iterative practices of Sprint Review and Retrospective drive continuous improvement in Agile projects, helping with product evolution and process refinement. By implementing insights gained and fostering a culture of learning and improvement, teams can sustain innovation and excellence in a competitive environment, delivering high-quality products effectively and with agility.

6.1: Product Backlog - Understanding and managing the product backlog.

The product backlog is a fundamental component of Agile and Scrum methodologies, serving as a dynamic and prioritised list of everything that might be needed in the product. It is more than just a list of tasks; it is a comprehensive inventory that provides a single source of truth for all project requirements, changes, and enhancements. Effective management of the product backlog is crucial for the success of a project, ensuring that it not only meets the current market demands but also adapts to changes swiftly and efficiently.

Understanding the Product Backlog

Definition and Purpose

A product backlog consists of items that could include new features, fixes, enhancements, and other activities necessary to achieve a particular product vision. It is the primary repository for all requirements targeting an upcoming release, managed and prioritised by the Product Owner. The main purpose of the product backlog is to keep the team aware of the tasks that need to be completed.

Composition of the Product Backlog

Backlog items, often referred to as User Stories, are typically written from the perspective of the user and include details necessary for the development team to understand the requirements. Items in the backlog are expressed in a way that is clear and measurable. They are prioritised based on a variety of factors, including business value, regulatory mandates, dependencies, and technical complexity.

Attributes of Product Backlog Items (PBIs)

Each item in the product backlog should possess certain attributes such as:
Description: What needs to be done?
Value:What is the expected benefit?
Estimates: How much effort is required?
Priority: What is the importance relative to other items?
Acceptance Criteria : Criteria to be applied to the delivered feature allowing it to be acceppted.

MCAREL Consulting
Superior Advisory Services for Guidewire Customers

Managing the Product Backlog

Backlog Grooming (Refinement)

Regular backlog grooming sessions, also known as backlog refinement, are essential. During these sessions, the Product Owner and the development team review items on the backlog to ensure clarity and relevance. This process includes adding detail, estimates, and order to items in the backlog. Refinement ensures that the backlog remains organised, relevant, and progressively detailed.

Prioritisation Techniques

Effective backlog management relies heavily on prioritisation. Several techniques can be employed, such as MoSCoW (Must have, Should have, Could have, and Won't have this time), the Kano model (categorising features based on customer satisfaction and investment), or value versus complexity matrices. Prioritisation is dynamic and should reflect changes in business objectives and market conditions.

Sprint Planning

During sprint planning, the team selects items from the product backlog they can complete during the coming sprint. The selection is based on the item's priority and the team's velocity or capacity. This process involves cooperative discussion between the Product Owner, who has a vision of what needs to be built, and the development team, who brings insights into the technical aspects of the project.

Transparency and Visibility

Maintaining transparency in the product backlog is crucial. All stakeholders should have access to view the backlog and understand the status of product development. This transparency ensures that everyone involved has a clear understanding of project priorities and progress.

Adaptation to Change

The product backlog is not static; it evolves with the project. It should be responsive to feedback from stakeholders, changes in the market, and insights gained by the development team during the development process. This flexibility helps in managing emerging requirements and adapting to changes without losing sight of the project goals.

Conclusion

The product backlog is more than just a list; it is a strategic tool in the Agile project management arsenal. Effective management of the product backlog ensures that the development team is focused, efficient, and aligned with the project goals and customer needs. It involves continuous evaluation, prioritisation, and refinement to ensure that every sprint delivers value to the business. Understanding and managing the product backlog effectively can dramatically improve the outcomes of a project, making it more responsive and successful in a competitive environment.

Recap

Product Backlog: Understanding and Managing the Product Backlog

The product backlog is a fundamental component of Agile and Scrum methodologies, serving as a dynamic and prioritised list of everything that might be needed in the product. It is more than just a list of tasks; it is a comprehensive inventory that provides a single source of truth for all project requirements, changes, and enhancements. Effective management of the product backlog is crucial for the success of a project, ensuring that it not only meets the current market demands but also adapts to changes swiftly and efficiently.

Understanding the Product Backlog

1. Definition and Purpose
2. A product backlog consists of items that could include new features, fixes, enhancements, and other activities necessary to achieve a particular product vision. It is the primary repository for all requirements targeting an upcoming release, managed and prioritised by the Product Owner. The main purpose of the product backlog is to keep the team aware of the tasks that need to be completed.
3. Composition of the Product Backlog
4. Backlog items, often referred to as User Stories, are typically written from the perspective of the user and include details necessary for the development team to understand the requirements. Items in the backlog are expressed in a way that is clear and measurable. They are prioritised based on a variety of factors, including business value, regulatory mandates, dependencies, and technical complexity.
5. Attributes of Product Backlog Items (PBIs)
6. Each item in the product backlog should possess certain attributes such as:

- Description: What needs to be done?
- Value: What is the expected benefit?
- Estimates: How much effort is required?
- Priority: What is the importance relative to other items?

Managing the Product Backlog

MCAREL Consulting
Superior Advisory Services for Guidance Customers

1. Backlog Grooming (Refinement)
2. Regular backlog grooming sessions, also known as backlog refinement, are essential. During these sessions, the Product Owner and the development team review items on the backlog to ensure clarity and relevance. This process includes adding detail, estimates, and order to items in the backlog. Refinement ensures that the backlog remains organised, relevant, and progressively detailed.
3. Prioritisation Techniques
4. Effective backlog management relies heavily on prioritisation. Several techniques can be employed, such as MoSCoW (Must have, Should have, Could have, and Won't have this time), the Kano model (categorising features based on customer satisfaction and investment), or value versus complexity matrices. Prioritisation is dynamic and should reflect changes in business objectives and market conditions.
5. Sprint Planning
6. During sprint planning, the team selects items from the product backlog they can complete during the coming sprint. The selection is based on the item's priority and the team's velocity or capacity. This process involves cooperative discussion between the Product Owner, who has a vision of what needs to be built, and the development team, who brings insights into the technical aspects of the project.
7. Transparency and Visibility
8. Maintaining transparency in the product backlog is crucial. All stakeholders should have access to view the backlog and understand the status of product development. This transparency ensures that everyone involved has a clear understanding of project priorities and progress.
9. Adaptation to Change
10. The product backlog is not static; it evolves with the project. It should be responsive to feedback from stakeholders, changes in the market, and insights gained by the development team during the development process. This flexibility helps in managing emerging requirements and adapting to changes without losing sight of the project goals.

Conclusion

The product backlog is more than just a list; it is a strategic tool in the Agile project management arsenal. Effective management of the product backlog ensures that the development team is focused, efficient, and aligned with the project goals and customer needs. It involves continuous evaluation, prioritisation, and refinement to ensure that every sprint delivers value to the business. Understanding and managing the product backlog effectively can dramatically improve

6.2: Sprint Backlog - Detailed exploration of the sprint backlog's role in sprint planning.

In Agile project management, particularly within the Scrum framework, the sprint backlog plays a critical role in sprint planning, acting as the bridge between the product backlog and the actual work done during a sprint. This section provides a detailed exploration of how the sprint backlog functions and its importance in sprint planning.

Definition and Purpose of the Sprint Backlog

The sprint backlog is a subset of the product backlog. It includes all tasks, requirements, and work that the development team commits to complete during a specific sprint. Unlike the product backlog, which is a broader list managed by the Product Owner, the sprint backlog is dynamic and continually updated by the team throughout the sprint. The main purpose of the sprint backlog is to provide a clear, detailed view of the work that needs to be accomplished during the sprint to reach the sprint goals.

Components of the Sprint Backlog

The sprint backlog typically contains:

User Stories:

Detailed requirements or features that are selected from the product backlog.

Tasks:

Breakdowns of each user story into manageable units of work, often estimated in hours.

Bugs/Fixes:

Identified issues from previous sprints or during the current sprint that need resolution.

Technical Debt:

Tasks aimed at resolving accumulated technical compromises that can affect code quality or project progress.

Each component is essential as it contributes directly to the sprint's deliverables, ensuring that the team focuses on both value delivery and quality.

MCAREL Consulting
Superior Advisory Services for Ou dew re Custe hers

Role in Sprint Planning

Task Identification and Assignment

In the courae of sprint planning, the team picks items from the product backlog to be moved into the sprint backlog. This process involves detailed discussions about the complexity, dependencies, and effort required for each task. The team then breaks down the user stories into specific tasks and assigns them to team members, making sure everyone understands their responsibilities.

Estimation and Resource Allocation

Tasks in the sprint backlog are estimated, usually in hours or days. This estimation helps in assessing the team's capacity and aids in effective resource allocation. Estimations can be refined throughout the sprint as more information becomes available or when unexpected challenges arise. The a subtle difference between stories and tasks. Stories always aim to provide requirements for a working feature or capability that can be released to the customer. Task are usually associated with a stories and these list the things that need to be done in order to complete the functionality and get it released to the customer. Some projects have a list of standard tasks called the definition of done that list ancilliary tasks that need to be completed before the code can be released to the customer.

Ensuring Flexibility and Adaptability:

The sprint backlog is not static; it is expected to evolve as the sprint progresses. The team may encounter unforeseen challenges or changes in scope, which may require adjustments to the backlog. This flexibility is crucial for maintaining the agility needed to respond to changes effectively.

Monitoring Progress

The sprint backlog is a critical tool for daily scrum meetings, where the team reviews progress and addresses any blockers. It provides a clear indication of what has been done, what is in progress, and what is yet to be started, facilitating better decision-making and adjustments.

Importance in Achieving Sprint Goals

The sprint backlog is instrumental in ensuring that the team remains on track and aligned with the sprint's objectives. It acts as a day-to-day guide for the development team, outlining the work and the sequence in which it should be tackled. Effective management of the sprint backlog is crucial for the team to deliver the planned increment within the constraints of time and quality.

In conclusion, the sprint backlog is more than just a list of tasks; it is a strategic tool that guides the team through the sprint. It guarantees that the whole team is on the same page and working together towards a common goal. Managing the sprint backlog effectively is vital for the success of the sprint, helping the team to deliver value consistently and adapt to changes swiftly.

MCAREL Consulting
Superior Advisory Services for Guidance to Customers

Recap

Welcome to the detailed exploration of the Sprint Backlog's role in Sprint Planning in Agile Project Management, particularly within the Scrum framework. The Sprint Backlog acts as a crucial bridge between the product backlog and the actual work conducted during a Sprint.

Definition and Purpose of the Sprint Backlog

- The Sprint Backlog, a subset of the Product Backlog, encompasses all tasks, requirements, and work the development team commits to completing during a specific Sprint. It is dynamic and continuously updated throughout the Sprint.
- The main purpose of the Sprint Backlog is to offer a clear, detailed view of the necessary work to achieve the Sprint goals.

Components of the Sprint Backlog

- User Stories: Detailed requirements or features selected from the Product Backlog.
- Tasks: Breakdowns of user stories into manageable units of work, often estimated in hours.
- Bugs/Fixes: Identified issues from previous or current Sprints requiring resolution.
- Technical Debt: Tasks that address accumulated technical compromises affecting code quality or project progress.

Role in Sprint Planning

1. Task Identification and Assignment: During Sprint planning, the team selects items from the Product Backlog to transition to the Sprint Backlog, followed by in-depth discussions to assess complexity, dependencies, and effort for each task. Tasks are then allocated to team members.
2. Estimation and Resource Allocation: Tasks in the Sprint Backlog are estimated (in hours or days) to evaluate the team's capacity and facilitate resource allocation. Estimations may be refined as new information surfaces or unexpected challenges arise.
3. Flexibility and Adaptability: The Sprint Backlog evolves throughout the Sprint to accommodate unforeseen challenges or scope changes, preserving agility for effective responses to modification.
4. Monitoring Progress: The Sprint Backlog is instrumental in daily Scrum meetings, providing a comprehensive overview of completed work, tasks in progress, and upcoming activities, aiding better decision-making and adjustment.

Importance in Achieving Sprint Goals

The Sprint Backlog is pivotal for aligning the team's efforts with the Sprint objectives, serving as a guide for day-to-day activities. Effective management ensures timely and high-quality delivery of the planned increment.

To summarize, the Sprint Backlog goes beyond being a mere list of tasks; it strategically navigates the team through the Sprint, uniting them towards shared goals. Well-orchestrated Sprint Backlog management is fundamental for Sprint success, enabling consistent value delivery and swift adaptation to changes.

6.3: Increment – The outcome of a sprint and its importance in the Scrum process.

In Scrum, an "Increment" refers to the tangible output of a sprint, the shortest, consistent, repeatable period during which a team works to complete set items from the product backlog. Understanding the role of the increment is crucial, as it encapsulates the essence of progress within the Scrum framework. This section explores the concept of the increment, its significance in the Scrum process, and how it helps teams deliver value consistently and efficiently.

Definition and Nature of the Increment

An increment in Scrum is the sum of all product backlog items completed during a sprint. The completed items are integrated with the work from the previous sprints.The increment is a step towards the final product, embodying all completed features that are "Done," meaning they meet a predefined standard of completion. This standard is often defined by the team's "Definition of Done," which ensures quality and completeness. Each increment must be in a usable condition regardless of whether the product owner decides to release it, maintaining Scrum's emphasis on delivering potentially shippable product segments at the end of every sprint.

Purpose of the Increment

The primary purpose of the increment is to produce a concrete, workable section of the product that adds value to the user or customer with each sprint. By doing so, Scrum allows for regular feedback and iterations, which are vital for adaptive and responsive product development. The increment serves as a critical feedback loop for the team, stakeholders, and clients, enabling them to see progress in real time and adjust the product direction based on working software rather than just documentation or plans.

The Role of the Increment in the Scrum Process

Transparency and Inspection: as discussed in earlier lessons. In Scrum, transparency is a foundational principle, and the increment is a tool that fosters this transparency. It allows stakeholders to inspect the actual state of the product at the end of every sprint, making the Scrum principles of inspection and adaptation feasible. Stakeholders can gauge the product's evolution and functionality through these increments.

Feedback and Adaptation

Each increment invites feedback from users and stakeholders, which is vital for the iterative improvement of the product. Feedback based on the actual use and functionality of the product can lead to valuable insights, which are incorporated into the next sprint planning session. This ensures that the product evolves in the right direction and that any adjustments needed are made promptly, thereby avoiding the pitfalls of waterfall methodologies.

Risk Management

Frequent increments also mean frequent risk assessments. Since the product is evaluated at the end of each sprint, risks associated with product development are identified and mitigated early. This not only saves time and resources but also ensures that the project aligns more closely with user expectations and market needs.

Motivation and Satisfaction

For development teams, the completion of an increment provides a sense of achievement and motivation. Seeing a working part of the product come to life after each sprint boosts morale and enhances productivity. For the product owner and stakeholders, it provides reassurance that their investment is yielding visible results, thus fostering greater satisfaction with the development process.

MCAREL Consulting
Superior Advisory Services for Guidewire Customers

Challenges with Increments

While the concept of delivering increments is robust, its implementation can face several challenges:

Maintaining Quality

Ensuring each increment is truly "Done" and meets the team's "Definition of Done" can be demanding. This often requires rigorous testing, integration, and review processes.

Integration Issues

As new functionalities are added, integrating these with existing increments can pose technical challenges, especially if the increments were not perfectly aligned or if architectural changes are needed.

Stakeholder Expectations

Sometimes, stakeholders may have expectations for faster delivery of more comprehensive features within each increment, which might not always be realistic within the time constraints of a sprint.

Conclusion

In conclusion, the increment is more than just an outcome of a sprint; it is a strategic tool within the Scrum framework that drives the iterative, incremental, and evolutionary nature of agile product development. In addition to giving the team a forum for feedback and ongoing adaptation based on actual user and business needs, it guarantees that the team stays committed to delivering value consistently. By understanding and effectively managing increments, Scrum teams can enhance their processes, deliver higher quality products, and ensure that they are meeting the expectations of all stakeholders involved. Through this approach, Scrum supports not only the logistical aspects of project management but also the broader goals of business strategy and customer satisfaction.

Recap

The product backlog is a crucial part of Agile and Scrum methodologies. It serves as a dynamic list of everything needed in a product, going beyond just tasks to encompass requirements, changes, and enhancements for the project. Effective management of the product backlog is essential for project success, ensuring it meets market demands and adapts swiftly to changes.

- Definition and Purpose: The product backlog consists of items like new features, fixes, enhancements, and activities needed for a product vision. It is the central repository for requirements managed and prioritized by the product owner.
- Composition: Backlog items, or user stories, are written from the user's perspective with clear details and measurability. They are prioritized based on factors like business value, dependencies, and complexity.
- Attributes of Product Backlog Items (PBIs): Each item should have a description, value, estimate, priority, and details on what needs to be done.

Proper management of the product backlog involves activities like backlog grooming, prioritization techniques, sprint planning, transparency, and adaptation to change.

- Backlog Grooming: Regular sessions ensure clarity and relevance by adding detail, estimates, and order to backlog items.
- Techniques for Prioritizing the Backlog: Methods like Moscow, Cano model, or value versus complexity matrices help in effective prioritization.
- Sprint Planning: Involves selecting backlog items for the upcoming sprint based on priority and team capacity, creating a sprint backlog.
- Transparency and Visibility: All stakeholders should have access to view the backlog, ensuring clear understanding of project priorities and progress.
- Adaptation to Change: The product backlog should evolve with feedback, market changes, and insights, adapting to emerging requirements without losing sight of project goals.

The increment in Scrum represents the tangible output of a sprint, encapsulating progress within the framework. It consists of all completed backlog items integrated from previous sprints, aiming to deliver potentially shippable product segments after each sprint.

- Definition and Nature: An increment is a step towards the final product, embodying completed features meeting a predefined standard of completion. It must be usable even if not released, ensuring quality and completeness.
- Purpose: It produces workable sections adding value to users with each sprint, facilitating feedback, iterations, and adaptive product development.
- Role in the Scrum Process: Offers transparency, feedback, risk management, and motivation for teams, stakeholders, and clients, ensuring satisfaction and iterative improvements.

Challenges with increments may include maintaining quality, integration issues, and managing stakeholder expectations for faster, comprehensive features. Effectively managing increments enhances Scrum processes, enabling higher quality products, and meeting stakeholder expectations consistently.

MCAREL Consulting
Superior Advisory Services for Guidew re Custo ner

7.1: Effective Sprint Planning - Techniques for successful sprint planning, including estimation and prioritisation.

By the end of this section, you'll be well-versed in advanced techniques for sprint planning, focusing particularly on the arts of estimation and prioritisation, ensuring your sprints not only start off on the right foot but also lead to successful outcomes.

MCAREL Consulting
Superior Advisory services for modern customers

Introduction

Sprint planning is more than just a preliminary step in Agile and Scrum; it's a crucial phase where your team aligns on the vision for the upcoming sprint. It determines what will be delivered and how. Today, we'll dive deep into effective, actionable strategies to enhance this process, focusing on making your estimation and prioritisation both efficient and accurate. It should be noted, however, that estimation is a controversial topic in some agile circles. Even to the point that some are advocating no estimates, others are suggesting story points are now outdated.

The essence of Sprint Planning

Sprint planning sets the stage for a successful sprint. It answers two fundamental questions:
What are we going to achieve in this sprint?
How will we achieve these goals?
This session involves the whole team: the Product Owner, who brings the vision; the Scrum Master, who facilitates; and the Development Team, who will be doing the work. It's crucial that everyone is on the same page regarding the sprint's objectives and the approach to accomplishing them.

Mastering Estimation

Accurate estimation is key to setting realistic sprint goals. Here are some techniques that have proven effective across various teams and projects:

Planning Poker

This gamified approach to estimation avoids the influence of the loudest voice in the room by having team members use numbered cards to vote on task sizes. It's fun and democratic, and it often leads to surprisingly accurate estimates because it combines diverse viewpoints. The estimates produced are usually defined in story points.

T-Shirt Sizing

MCAREL Consulting
Superior Advisory services for Guidewire Customers

This technique uses relative sizing (XS, S, M, L, XL) to categorise tasks by complexity rather than exact time frames. It's particularly useful when the team needs to quickly sort a large backlog into manageable segments. Again, this can be utilised with story points and each size is assigned a value; for example,

XS =. 1 point,

S=3,

M =5,

L=8,

XL = 13.

As we can see, 13 is the biggest and could probably be squeezed into a 3-week sprint. Anything bigger than that is often put through a levelling or slicing process aimed at splitting the story into multiple smaller stories that fit into a single sprint.

Affinity Estimating

A collaborative sorting activity where tasks are arranged on a wall or table from smallest to largest. Teams discuss and categorise tasks together, which builds understanding and consensus on the workload and complexity.

1. Prioritisation Techniques

With tasks estimated, prioritisation determines the order of execution, ensuring that resources are allocated to maximise value. Here's how to do it right:

MoSCoW Method

By categorising tasks into must-have, should-have, could-have, and won't-have, this method ensures focus remains on essential deliverables, helping manage scope and stakeholder expectations effectively.

Value vs. Effort Matrix

This approach involves plotting tasks on a grid based on the effort they require versus the value they provide. Tasks in the high-value, low-effort quadrant are tackled first to maximise impact with minimal resources.

Kano Model

This model helps categorise features based on customer satisfaction and functionality. Features are split into the following categories:

- basic,
- performance,
- excitement,
- indifference.

It's especially useful for product-driven teams focused on user experience.

Weighted Shortest Job First (WSJF)

Used in SAFe (Scaled Agile Framework), this method calculates task priority based on cost of delay and job size. It's excellent for environments where delay costs are significant.

1. Overcoming Common Sprint Planning Challenges

Overcommitment

Use velocity and historical performance as benchmarks to set realistic goals. Over commitment can be a huge problem. Regularly missing your sprint goals can reduce stackholder confidence and put the whole project at risk. Over achieving in relation to your goals is always well received. When defining your goals be conservative, define the goal as the minimum viable implementation of the feature, use stretch goals to enhance the feature beyond the minimum requirement.

Vague User Stories

Collaborate with the product owner to refine stories so they are actionable and testable. Make sure concrete acceptance criteria are defined for each story. If necessary, hold the three amigos meeting with the developer, business analyst or product owner, and tester to discuss how you're going to move forward with the feature and whether there are any gaps in the information that you require.

External Dependencies

Identify potential blockers early and devise contingency plans. When planning, be sure to account for dependencies. Features may not meet the minimum requirement, for example, because the integrations are not available.

1. Enhancing Your Toolbox with Digital Aids:

Project Management Tools: You can define your backlog and user stories in spreadsheets and put them on the shared drive if you want to. However, there is a wealth of agile project management tools out there with direct support for:

- User Stories
- Product backlog
- Sprint backlog
- Sprints
- Kanban boards
- Story Point
- Estimated hours
- Actual hours etc.

That allows you to do most of your work within the tool and provides flexible reporting options.

Examples include, tools like JIRA, Trello, and Asana are invaluable for visualising and tracking progress.

Remote Planning Software: Online tools like PlanITpoker and FunRetro facilitate digital Planning Poker sessions, making remote estimations seamless.

Conclusion:

Effective sprint planning transforms good teams into great ones by setting a clear, achievable path forward each sprint. Through precise estimation and strategic prioritisation, your team can deliver consistent value, adapting swiftly to changing needs and ensuring stakeholder satisfaction.

Note, as I mentioned earlier, some of these practices are viewed as obsolete, and some Agile practitioners decry estimates altogether. But the reality is you find projects at different points on the agile evolutionary timeline and will probably find projects using points and or doing big upfront estimates and being successful with those approaches. It's also worth noting that even the no-estimates brigade still use techniques like story slicing which intrinsically sizes stories and by default is a form of estimate and relative measure. I you're joining a sucessfull existing project there's no need to change. If you're joining a new project then it's probably best to use the most current thinking. If you need a big upfront estimate for commercial reasons, try and make sure you have enough empirical data to support it.

MCAREL Consulting
Superior Advisory services for Guidewire customers

Recap

Effective Sprint Planning focuses on successful techniques including estimation and prioritization. The learning objectives cover advanced techniques in estimation and prioritization for achieving successful outcomes in sprints.

- Introduction: Sprint planning in Agile and Scrum is a crucial phase determining what will be delivered and how. The session involves the Product Owner, Scrum Master, and Development Team aligning on the sprint's objectives.
- The Essence of Sprint Planning: It sets the stage for a successful sprint by answering questions on goals and approach. Involves the whole team to ensure a shared understanding.
- Mastering Estimation:
    - Planning Poker: A gamified approach to estimation using numbered cards, enhancing accuracy.
    - T-Shirt Sizing: Categorizing tasks by complexity rather than timeframes, aiding backlog management.
    - Affinity Estimating: Collaborative sorting to build consensus on workload and complexity.
- Prioritization Techniques:
    - MoSCoW Method: Categorizes tasks into must-have, should-have, could-have, and won't-have for focus on essential deliverables.
    - Value vs. Effort Matrix: Prioritizing tasks based on value and effort, ensuring high impact with minimal resources.
    - Kano Model: Helps categorize features based on customer satisfaction and functionality.
    - Weighted Shortest Job First (WSJF): Prioritization based on cost of delay and job size, useful in significant delay cost environments.
- Common Sprint Planning Challenges: Covers overcommitment, vague user stories, and managing external dependencies to ensure realistic goals and stakeholder satisfaction.
- Enhancing Your Toolbox with Digital Aids: Project management tools like JIRA, Trello, and Asana support agile project management effectively. Remote planning software such as PlanITpoker and FunRetro facilitate digital sessions.
- Conclusion: Effective Sprint Planning with precise estimation and prioritization ensures consistent value delivery, swift adaptation to changing needs, and stakeholder satisfaction.

7.2: Sprint Execution -
Best practices for executing sprints, maintaining momentum, and ensuring continuous delivery.

7.2: Sprint Execution - Best Practices

Sprint Execution in Scrum, particularly in software development, is a critical phase where teams turn ideas into functional outputs. This phase, characterized by "sprinting", focuses on maintaining a laser-sharp focus on the current set of goals to avoid distractions and ensure continuous delivery. Here, sprinting implies a concentrated effort during a set time frame (usually two to four weeks), aimed at completing specific, pre-defined tasks.
Best Practices for Executing Sprints

Fostering a Collaborative Working Environment:

Co-located Teams: Having team members work in close physical proximity can significantly enhance communication and collaboration. Co-location supports spontaneous meetings, quick resolution of issues, and more dynamic teamwork. It naturally fosters a team environment where members can synergize their efforts effectively.
Tools for Remote Teams: For remote teams, leveraging tools like Slack, Microsoft Teams, and Zoom helps mitigate communication challenges. These tools enable real-time chatting, video calls, and screen sharing, bridging the gap caused by physical distance. Additionally, using agile project management tools such as Jira, Trello, or Asana can keep everyone on the same page regarding sprint progress and task distribution.

Maintaining Momentum

- **Daily Stand-Ups:** These short, daily meetings are crucial for maintaining sprint momentum. They serve to inform everyone about what was accomplished the day before, the goals for the current day, and any obstacles that might impede progress.

MCAREL Consulting
Superior Advisory Services for our dear customers

- **Sprint Retrospectives**: Held at the end of each sprint, retrospectives allow the team to reflect on what went well and what didn't. This meeting is essential for iterative improvement, ensuring that each sprint is more effective than the last.
3. Ensuring Continuous Delivery:

Ensuring Continuous Delivery

Continuous Integration/Continuous Deployment (CI/CD): Implementing CI/CD practices ensures that changes to the software are automatically tested and deployed, reducing the time to release and increasing the quality of the software.
Feature Toggling: This technique allows teams to merge and deploy features into the main branch without making them visible to users until they are ready. Feature toggles facilitate continuous delivery and A/B testing.

Enhancing Transparency

Visible Task Boards: Digital or physical task boards should be updated in real-time to reflect current sprint status. This visibility ensures that every team member and stakeholder understands the progress and challenges.
Open Sprint Reviews: Inviting stakeholders to sprint reviews promotes transparency. During these sessions, the team demonstrates new features and discusses the next steps. This practice not only keeps the stakeholders informed but also ensures that the product aligns with their expectations.

Interaction with Business Stakeholders

Regular Engagement: Ensuring that business stakeholders are regularly engaged with the sprint's progress helps in aligning the development work with business needs. Frequent interactions can help in gathering feedback early and adjusting plans accordingly.

Using Tools to Support the Process:

- **Integration Tools:** Tools that integrate with the team's existing workflows (like GitHub, Bitbucket for code repositories) can enhance efficiency. Automation tools can also be set up to handle repetitive tasks, allowing the team to focus more on creative problem-solving.
- **Analytics and Progress Tracking Tools:** Utilizing tools to track progress and analyze bottlenecks can significantly enhance the efficiency of sprint executions.

Conclusion

Executing sprints effectively requires a blend of the right practices, tools, and an environment conducive to agile development. Co-located teams can leverage their proximity for better synergy, while remote teams must effectively use communication tools to bridge any gaps. Continuous delivery can be supported through CI/CD practices and feature toggling, ensuring that the team can keep pace with the demands of the business environment. Ultimately, transparency, frequent stakeholder interaction, and the right tools are pivotal in maintaining the momentum and success of sprint executions. By adhering to these best practices, teams can ensure that their sprinting efforts are as productive and effective as possible.

Recap

Sprint Execution in Scrum is a critical phase where teams turn ideas into functional outputs through a concentrated effort aimed at completing specific tasks within a set time frame. There are best practices to follow to make the Sprint run smoothly:

- Fostering a collaborative working environment by having co-located teams and using tools like Slack or Jira for remote teams.
- Maintaining momentum through daily stand-ups and Sprint retrospectives.
- Ensuring continuous delivery with practices like CI/CD and feature toggling.
- Enhancing transparency using visible task boards and open Sprint reviews.
- Interacting with business stakeholders regularly to align development with business needs.
- Using tools like integration tools, automation tools, and analytics to support the Sprint process.

By adhering to these best practices, teams can ensure that their Sprint executions are productive and effective, leading to successful outcomes.

Back Page Title

We wrote this book to help clarify the world of Scrum to the uninitiated. The Agile methodologies are evolving at pace and in the world of Linkedin and Facebook groups discussing Agile all seem to take differing views on what is right the way. This book aims to lead you through the minefield of Agile showing how straight forward running Agile projects can be, by helping the reader to understand concepts rather than following the methodolgy by rote. MCAREL Consulting are a small system integrator based on the Isle of Man. We have experience on Agile projects using Scrum for 20 years. We've seen successful use of Scrum on 30+ projects all of which have been run differently. The key is understanding the concepts and doing what works for your organisation. Good Luck !!

MCAREL Consulting
Superior Advisory Services for Guidance to customers